Letter from the Editor

Dear Readers,

We are very excited to welcome you all to Volume XI of The Arbitration Brief. The Arbitration Brief is a student publication of the American University Washington College of Law. The Arbitration Brief aims to become a leading academic publication for arbitration-related matters in the United States and abroad.

The Arbitration Brief is an entirely student-run organization. We publish articles submitted by professors, arbitrators, practitioners, and students alike. All articles are selected, edited, and published by the Brief's editorial board and staff.

The Arbitration Brief would like to thank the authors of this issue for their patience, responsiveness, and cooperation with our editorial board throughout the editing process. The Arbitration Brief would like to express its deep gratitude to the International Center on Commercial Arbitration, without which this publication would not have been possible. Last of all, I would personally like to thank the Brief's staff for their exceptional editing and tireless work ethic that has culminated in this issue.

Please explore our website for more information about The Arbitration Brief. If you have any questions, please feel free to reach out to arbitrationbrief@wcl.american.edu.

Best Regards,

Angelica Marisa Littlefield
Editor-in-Chief
Volume XI

THE ARBITRATION BRIEF

Volume XI

The Arbitration Brief is a student publication of American University Washington College of Law prepared with the assistance of the Washington College of Law Center on International Commercial Arbitration. The mission of this publication is to provide timely information, both practical and academic, on developments in the field of arbitration. We welcome pieces from academics, practicing attorneys, arbitrators, and students. For more information, please contact arbitrationbrief@wcl.american.edu. The views expressed in this publication are those of the writers and are not necessarily those of the editors, the Center on International Commercial Arbitration, or American University.

THE ARBITRATION BRIEF
2023-2024

EDITOR-IN-CHIEF
Angelica Marisa Littlefield

MANAGING ARTICLE EDITOR	**MANAGING DIGITAL EDITOR**
Gabrielle Scanlin-Sherman	Colin McGinness

SENIOR ARTICLE EDITORS
Marimar Seda Alvarez   Nathaniel Chaij

ARTICLE EDITORS

Aissatou Toure	Dominic Charles
Benin Lee	Jake Helfant

SENIOR STAFF

Scarlett Horn	Savannah Kelly
Abby Hug	Yonah Wasik
Gemma Muirhead	Jacqueline Vanacore
Lucas Vieweg	Deborah Slattery-Pereira
Nguyet Le	

JUNIOR STAFF

Amy Liu	Kaley Gilbert	Erin Moloney
Brian Hwang	Adam Bear	Hanadi Saidoun
Caitlen Moser	Jason Kehoe	Isha Jadhav
Emily Granja	Nathan Yost	Philip Winkle
Erik Romanin	Patrick Dumitrescu	Shannon Moloney

TABLE OF CONTENTS

Arbitration and the Energy Sector: Shifting Towards Efficiency..........................1
Jocelyn Absher

On the Court and International Arbitration at the Astana International Financial Center for Foreign Investors in the Oil and Gas Industry..................36
Shalala Valiyeva

Will European Withdrawal from the Energy Charter Treaty Be a Setback for Investments in the Region? The Future of Investment Arbitration in Europe and Remedies for a Potential Crisis of Justice...64
Weronika Rydzińska

Goldman Sachs 1MDB Arbitration..98
Benin Lee

Navigating Policy Shifts in Investor-State Dispute Settlement in Latin America: A Case Study of Colombia..103
Jake Helfant

Arbitration at the ILO: A New Mechanism..107
Yonah Wasik

ARBITRATION AND THE ENERGY SECTOR: SHIFTING TOWARDS EFFICIENCY

JOCELYN ABSHER*

ABSTRACT

While international arbitration remains the most common dispute-resolution mechanism used across international energy projects, there have been recent criticisms of its efficiency. An arbitration proceeding generally offers quicker results than traditional litigation, but those proceedings can frustrate the already lengthy timelines of construction contracts in renewable energy projects, such as an offshore wind farm which can take between five (5) to ten (10) years to develop[1] according to the World Bank. As the demand for energy efficiency and energy security continues to rise, the legal frameworks in international arbitration need to match the demand for evolution. A mechanism referred to as Dispute Adjudication Boards ("DABs") has shown historical success by swiftly resolving disputes and allowing construction projects to carry on. This article discusses the international legal frameworks and dispute resolution mechanisms that guide the future development of renewable energy projects and the resolution of inevitable disputes.

---

*Jocelyn Absher is an alumnus of American University Washington College of Law, Class of 2022. She holds a Master of Laws (LLM) degree with a Specialization in Arbitration from Bucerius Law School in Hamburg, Germany.

---

[1] *Expanding Offshore Wind to Emerging Markets*, WORLD BANK (Oct. 31, 2019), https://www.worldbank.org/en/topic/energy/publication/expanding-offshore-wind-in-emerging-markets.

1. INTRODUCTION 3
   A. The Energy Sector and International Arbitration 3
2. BACKGROUND INFORMATION 5
   A. Overview of Dispute Resolution Mechanisms 5
   B. A Comparison: Arbitration vs. Adjudication 6
   C. A Need for Dispute Adjudication Boards 7
   D. So Why Dispute Boards? 8
3. OVERVIEW OF MAIN INSTITUTIONS AND INSTRUMENTS THAT PLAY A ROLE 10
   A. A Comparison: Investment Arbitration vs. Commercial Arbitration 11
   B. UNCITRAL 13
   C. ICC 15
   D. The New York Convention 16
   E. FIDIC 17
      i. Overview of FIDIC Legal Frameworks 19
4. LEGAL ASPECTS OF DISPUTE BOARDS 21
   A. How Do Dispute Boards Work? 21
   B. Different Forms of Boards: Standing vs. Ad Hoc 22
      i. Standing 22
      ii. Ad Hoc 22
   C. Rules of Procedure: Examination of the Governing Rules and Guidelines 22
   D. Constituting the Dispute Board 23
   E. Decision-making Process: Evaluation of the Process Followed by Dispute Boards in Reaching Decisions 24
   F. Where a Dispute Board Decision is a Condition Precedent to Arbitration 27
   G. Enforcement of a DAAB's Decision 28
   H. Dissatisfaction with DAAB's Decision 28
   I. Effectiveness of Decisions 29
   J. Some Criticisms 29
5. CHARACTERISTIC CONSIDERATIONS OF RENEWABLE ENERGY PROJECTS 30
6. LOOKING FORWARD 31
7. CONCLUSIONS 32

1. **INTRODUCTION**

A. **The Energy Sector and International Arbitration**

Climate change is a global issue, and global efforts have intensified to become climate-neutral by 2050. The core to climate change solutions is reducing greenhouse gas emissions, which can be done by reducing non-renewable sources and investing in renewables. Switching our primary energy sources to clean and renewable energy is the best way to scale back on fossil fuel use. This transition is essential not only for decarbonization and significant reductions in carbon dioxide ("CO2") emissions to align with global net-zero goals,[2] but also to promote energy security. Given the surge in global energy prices caused by post-COVID demand and the ongoing conflict in Ukraine, accelerating the transition towards non-fossil fuel energy sources is becoming increasingly time-sensitive.[3]

The war in Ukraine rightfully struck the world with concern. In addition to being a human tragedy, the war shocked the global economy, and particularly the energy markets.[4] Regarding the energy industry, the executive director of the International Energy Agency ("IEA") released a statement in 2022 claiming that the world's "first truly global energy crisis"[5] may be the historical turning point that accelerates development toward energy security and sustainability. The executive director's statement was made following cuts to oil supply by major oil producers, tightened markets for liquefied natural gas, and a decision by the Organization of Petroleum Exporting Countries ("OPEC") to cut the output of millions of oil barrels per day.[6] However, this energy crisis is occurring at a time when the clean energy market is taking off.

A massive number of transactions occur in the energy industry every day, and arbitration of energy disputes is already commonplace in international law. With the increase in demand for energy resources, this area of law should continue to

---

[2] David Foxwell, *FIDIC Begins Work on New Contract Intended Specifically for Offshore Wind Projects*, RIVIERA (July 6, 2023), https://www.rivieramm.com/news-content-hub/news-content-hub/work-starts-on-new-fidic-contract-for-offshore-wind-projects-76836.
[3] *Id.*
[4] Óscar Arce, Gerrit Koester, & Christiane Nickel, *One Year since Russia's Invasion of Ukraine – the Effects on Euro Area Inflation*, THE ECB BLOG, EUROPEAN CENTRAL BANK (Feb. 24, 2023), https://www.ecb.europa.eu/press/blog/date/2023/html/ecb.blog20230224~3b753 62af3.en.html.
[5] *World Is in Its 'First Truly Global Energy Crisis', Says IEA's Birol*, EURACTIV (Oct. 25, 2022), https://www.euractiv.com/section/energy/news/world-is-in-its-first-truly-global-energy-crisis-says-ieas-birol/.
[6] *Id.*

evolve, especially considering that it is an industry characterized by unpredictability and substantial change. Compared to other industries, the energy market is susceptible to geographical, technical, political, and market risks;[7] these vulnerabilities are coupled with the intricate and capital-intensive nature of long-term development projects. The reality is that disputes are inevitable, but disputes can also be manageable with prudent resolution mechanisms in place.

The International Centre for Energy Arbitration posted a report that illustrates a firm preference for international energy actors to use international arbitration as their primary method of dispute resolution.[8] While domestic energy projects are normally litigated at the level of national courts, players within the international energy market seek to resolve disputes in forums where the substantive law and procedural rules will not be subject to bias or hostility. They strive to make contractual agreements that provide certainty "as to where and by whom their potential disputes may be resolved."[9] International arbitration is therefore the preferred mechanism to settle energy disputes in a neutral and customizable manner.

Practice reflects preference for arbitration, with the energy sector accounting for the vast majority of arbitrations heard under the International Center for Settlement of Investment Disputes ("ICSID") and for the second-largest area of disputes heard under the International Chamber of Commerce ("ICC").[10] Consequently, "energy arbitration" has emerged as its own area of practice with a growing group of industry-experienced and highly skilled practitioners.[11]

---

[7] *See generally* Simon Vorburger & Angelina M. Petti, *Chapter 11: Arbitrating Energy Disputes*, in ARBITRATION IN SWITZERLAND: THE PRACTITIONER'S GUIDE 1277–319 (2nd ed., ed. Manuel Arroyo, Alphen aan den Rijn: Kluwer Law International, 2018).

[8] *The Initial Report on Dispute Resolution in the Energy Sector*, INTERNATIONAL CENTRE FOR ENERGY ARBITRATION (ICEA) (May 2015), http://www.energyarbitration.org; *2013 International Arbitration Survey*, PWC AND QUEEN MARY UNIVERSITY OF LONDON, http://www.arbitration.qmul.ac.uk/research/2013/index.html (last visited July 16, 2023).

[9] *See generally* Simon Vorburger & Angelina M. Petti, *Chapter 11: Arbitrating Energy Disputes*, in ARBITRATION IN SWITZERLAND: THE PRACTITIONER'S GUIDE 1277–319 (2nd ed., ed. Manuel Arroyo, Alphen aan den Rijn: Kluwer Law International, 2018).

[10] ANNUAL REPORT 2023, INTERNATIONAL CENTRE FOR SETTLEMENT OF INVESTMENT DISPUTES 29 (2023), https://icsid.worldbank.org/sites/default/files/publications/ICSID_AR2023_ENGLISH_web_spread.pdf.

[11] *Id.*

2. BACKGROUND INFORMATION

A. Overview of Dispute Resolution Mechanisms

It is imperative parties plan for dispute resolution mechanisms before issues arise. Naturally, the choice of dispute resolution mechanism is highly dependent on the combination of relevant factors, such as the nature and complexity of a dispute, the contractual agreement, applicable laws, as well as the preferences of the parties involved. Commonly used dispute resolution mechanisms in the renewable energy sector include negotiation and mediation, dispute adjudication boards ("DABs"), arbitration, and litigation.[12] Generally, arbitration plays a role only after a dispute ripens, tolling the project participants because it damages the working relationships and the expenses incurred.

Negotiation is a preferred first step in resolving disputes in almost any situation since it involves direct discussions between parties to reach a mutually acceptable solution. However, negotiation is suitable primarily in straightforward situations where parties are willing to engage cooperatively. Often parties need a neutral third-party participant (such as a mediator) to facilitate negotiations between parties to arrive at a mutually acceptable resolution. Mediation, involving a middleman, is particularly useful when there are any complexities beyond the average person's experience or disconnects in communication.

Large-scale renewable energy projects widely use DABs.[13] DABs consist of impartial experts or lawyers that are appointed at the beginning of the project and provide ongoing assistance in resolving disputes that appear during the project's execution.[14] Such boards are preferable when disputes are anticipated during a project that requires ongoing expert involvement to render a timely resolution. If the board is unsuccessful at rendering a decision that both parties accept, that dispute will continue to arbitration or litigation depending on what the contract clause stipulates.

Arbitration is a more formal and binding option for dispute resolution. Arbitration involves presenting the dispute to one or more arbitrators who issue a final and binding decision (the "arbitral award").[15] Arbitration would be

---

[12] Kate Gough et al., *Resolving disputes on renewable energy projects – what tools are available and how do you choose?*, FRESHFIELDS BRUCKHAUS DERINGER (Apr. 22, 2022), https://sustainability.freshfields.com/post/102hn4t/resolving-disputes-on-renewable-energy-projects-what-tools-are-available-and-ho.

[13] *Id.*

[14] Matt Viator, *What Is a Dispute Resolution Board (DRB)?*, LEVELSET (Aug. 3, 2022), https://www.levelset.com/blog/what-is-a-dispute-resolution-board-drb/.

[15] *What is Arbitration?*, WIPO, https://www.wipo.int/amc/en/arbitration/what-is-arb.html#:~:text=...tion%20is%20a%20procedure%20in,instead%20of%20goin

preferable when parties desire a neutral and enforceable decision and want to avoid lengthy court proceedings. It is often used for disputes that involve complex legal and technical issues. Arbitration is also the leading dispute mechanism when confidentiality is important.[16]

In contrast, litigation resolves disputes in a public forum through courts and judicial proceedings.[17] Litigation may be necessary when alternative forms of dispute resolution (such as negotiation or mediation) are unsuccessful. Litigation can be suitable for complex and high-stakes disputes, such as those seen in the renewable energy sector, to proffer legal interpretation and create precedent-setting decisions.

B. A Comparison: Arbitration vs. Adjudication

A fundamental difference between an arbitral award and an adjudicatory decision is the long-term effect of those outcomes. There are four fundamental features of arbitration. They are: an alternative to national court; a private and confidential mechanism for dispute resolution; selected and controlled by the parties; with final and binding determinations of parties' rights and obligations.[18] When parties select arbitration to resolve disputes, those parties agree to give effect to that arbitral award and accept its finality, with only very limited exceptions to challenge it. Notably, arbitral awards are final and enforceable in most countries around the world due to the New York Convention.[19]

On the other hand, adjudication involves the resolution of disputes on an expedited basis. While it involves a binding decision, that decision is not necessarily final.[20] Adjudication serves as a form of interim dispute resolution, but it often functions to dispose of disputes and prevent further proceedings.[21] Adjudication is a frequent inclusion in construction or engineering contracts through the implementation of dispute boards; some jurisdictions, such as the

---

g%20to%20court (last visited June 4, 2024).

[16] GARY BORN, INTERNATIONAL COMMERCIAL ARBITRATION §20.01 (3d ed. 2023).

[17] *What are the Three Basic Types of Dispute Resolution? What to Know About Mediation, Arbitration, and Litigation*, PROGRAM ON NEGOTIATION HARVARD LAW SCHOOL (Dec. 1, 2023), https://www.pon.harvard.edu/daily/dispute-resolution/what-are-the-three-basic-types-of-dispute-resolution-what-to-know-about-mediation-arbitration-and-litigation/#:~:text=3.-,Litigation,evidence%20and%20making%20a%20ruling.

[18] JULIAN D.M. LEW, ET AL., COMPARATIVE INTERNATIONAL COMMERCIAL ARBITRATION 3 (The Hague: Kluwer Law International, 2003).

[19] UNITED NATIONS CONVENTION ON THE RECOGNITION AND ENFORCEMENT OF FOREIGN ARBITRAL AWARDS, art. 3, June 10, 1958, 330 U.N.T.S. 3.

[20] LEW, ET AL., *supra* note 18, at 3.

[21] *Id.*

United Kingdom, even require adjudication by statute for any contracts regarding construction.[22] The adjudicator is tasked to issue a decision in a short period expressly provided for in the agreement. That decision is then binding on the parties and immediately enforceable, but compared to arbitration, that decision may end up being an extra step in the dispute resolution process. While the adjudicator's decision is binding initially, parties can challenge it if either party is dissatisfied with that decision. The decision of an adjudicator "attains its finality only if not subsequently challenged, the timeline for challenge elapses, or the challenge is unsuccessful."[23] If challenged, the parties may ultimately resort to arbitration or litigation to determine their disputes more formally.

C. A Need for Dispute Adjudication Boards

Construction contracts are distinct as some of the most complex agreements within the realm of international trade law. These contracts span over extended periods and entail substantial investments in financial capital, technical expertise, and human resources. Disputes arising in construction contracts "create a substantial dilution of effort,"[24] which leads to decreased productivity, diversion of funds, and delayed project completion. Therefore, it is in the best interest of international stakeholders to swiftly minimize contractual disputes and the subsequent disruptions to the overall purpose and timeline of the projects. For this reason, the International Federation of Consulting Engineers ("FIDIC") proposed that such multi-party contracts use dispute boards to scale back the number of disputes that ultimately get referred to arbitration.[25]

An arbitral tribunal can exercise discretion at any time during a proceeding; however, the recent United Nations Commission on International Trade Law ("UNCITRAL") guidance texts encourage that tribunals exercise power early on since an underlying objective of international arbitration is to enhance the efficiency of arbitral proceedings.[26] The evolution of alternative dispute

---

[22] *Id.*

[23] United Nations General Assembly, *Settlement of Commercial Disputes, Adjudication, Note by the Secretariat*, ¶ 6, U.N. Doc. A/CN.9/WG.II/WP.225 (Jan. 27, 2022).

[24] *See* Peter O'Malley, *A New 'UNCITRAL Model Law on International Commercial Adjudication': How Beneficial Could It Really Be?*, 88 INTL. J. ARB., MEDIATION & DISP. MGMT. 34, 45 (Feb. 2022).

[25] PRACTICE NOTE I: DISPUTE AVOIDANCE-FOCUSING ON DISPUTE BOARDS, FIDIC DISPUTE AVOIDANCE AND ADJUDICATION FORUM 12 (2023), https://issuu.com/fidic/docs/2023_practice_note_on_dispute_avoidance_e-brochure?fr=xKAE9_zU1NQ.

[26] United Nations General Assembly, *Early dismissal and preliminary determination, Note by the Secretariat*, n.4 U.N. Doc. A/CN.9/1114 (Feb. 24,

resolution reveals a trend for more "flexible and informal mediation-like" dispute resolution procedures.[27] Since the initial success of the dispute board process with the Eisenhower Tunnel project, dispute resolution boards have grown in popularity.[28] Dispute boards have therefore become more "commonplace" in the international construction industry, which, like arbitration, also emerged in the 1960s. A dispute boards' first reported use was in the Boundary Dam project in Washington state.[29] That project tasked a technical "Joint Consulting Board" to make decisions and was "asked to continue its operation" throughout the project's development.[30]

Since the 1960s, standard forms of contracts emerged and empowered engineers with quasi-judicial roles to decide disputes, but suspicions grew over the "true independence" of these engineers as agents; meanwhile, costs to resolve claims through arbitration notably increased.[31] So, the need developed for a fair, timely, and cost-conscious system to resolve disputes, particularly between parties from different nationalities.[32]

D. So Why Dispute Boards?

Due to the use of dispute boards, approximately ninety-eight percent (98%) of disputes avoid litigation or arbitration.[33] Cases of international construction or infrastructure contracts commonly use them[34] since they can serve as early action alternatives to arbitration by providing determinations or recommendations to disputes without interrupting the performance of the contract. Dispute Boards are

---

2022).

[27] *See generally* Albert Bates & R. Zachary Torres-Fowler, *Dispute Boards: A Different Approach to Dispute Resolution*, in THE COMPARATIVE LAW YEARBOOK OF INTERNATIONAL BUSINESS 243 (Volume 41a: International Mediation, ed. Christian Campbell, Kluwer Law International, 2020).

[28] Fred Yavorsky, *The ABCs of DRBs. What They Are and How Well They Work*, CAPITAL PROJECT MANAGEMENT, INC. (May 26, 2016), https://cpmiteam.com/2006/03/the-abcs-of-drbs/.

[29] *Id.*

[30] P. H. J. Chapman et al., *Dispute Boards on Major Infrastructure Projects*, ICE PUBLISHING, PROCEEDINGS OF THE INSTITUTION OF CIVIL ENGINEERS - MANAGEMENT, PROCUREMENT AND LAW (May 25, 2015), https://www.icevirtuallibrary.com/doi/10.1680/mpal.2009.162.1.7.

[31] *Id.*

[32] *Id.*

[33] Matt Viator, *What Is a Dispute Resolution Board (DRB)?*, LEVELSET (Aug. 3, 2022), https://www.levelset.com/blog/what-is-a-dispute-resolution-board-drb/.

[34] Lindy Patterson & Nicholas Higgs, *Dispute Boards*, GLOBAL ARBITRATION REVIEW (Oct. 19, 2021), https://globalarbitrationreview.com/guide/the-guide-construction-arbitration/fourth-edition/article/dispute-boards#footnote-045.

particularly suitable for large-scale, long-term projects that involve complex engineering or construction over several years and are prone to disputes arising during their execution. The board's primary purpose is to assist in the resolution of disputes that arise between parties during the contract, so that parties "comply now, argue later."[35] By using dispute boards for renewable energy projects, expectations on how to approach disagreements are clear early on in a project's development. Proactively setting preventative measures in combination with communication and transparency achieves this.

The construction industry is highly susceptible to disputes for various reasons and it's infrequent that a construction project goes exactly as planned. Modifications to project plans are common practice, including a change in resources or capital to implement those modifications.[36] Disputes often arise regarding whether the constructor should receive additional payments for those changes and whether strict time schedules for project completion may lead to potentially high penalties for delays.[37] Within international business, construction, and legal communities, there is a growing narrative that the advantages of arbitration over litigation (namely time and cost efficiency) are waning.[38] This presents a need for new solutions. The parties to international construction contracts must have a mechanism to obtain binding decisions to resolve the disputes on an interim basis, thus allowing the project to continue. The solution is to use dispute boards, which contracts usually will empower. International construction contracts will address the above-mentioned concerns by including a provision that calls for dispute resolution boards to handle a contractual dispute as it arises.

Dispute boards serve as an intermediary for parties to resolve disputes before they grow to an undesirable level of formality. Since dispute boards can serve as a broad range of intermediaries, from mediators to arbiters, the boards operate as a unique hybrid tool to resolve disputes—which falls somewhere between

---

[35] *Id.*
[36] Michael Harris, *Why Construction Disputes Occur and How to Promote Early and Amicable Settlements*, LONG INTERNATIONAL, https://www.long-intl.com/articles/why-construction-disputes-occur/ (last visited Apr. 19, 2024).
[37] James Loftis et al., *Energy Sector Construction Disputes*, GLOBAL ARBITRATION REVIEW (Oct. 12, 2023), https://globalarbitrationreview.com/guide/the-guide-construction-arbitration/fifth-edition/article/energy-sector-construction-disputes.
[38] *See* Anton Maurer, *How International Commercial Arbitration Can Be More Efficient, Speedier, and Less Costly*, JAMS (Oct. 25, 2023), https://www.jamsadr.com/blog/2023/how-international-commercial-arbitration-can-be-more-efficient#_ftn1.

mediation and formal arbitration.[39] Normally, the board is set up at the time of contract formation has a "standing body . . . of one or three members"[40] who are well acquainted with the parties, the contract, and its purpose. Different kinds of panels are available for use by parties depending on the sort of power the parties wish to designate.

According to the ICC, dispute boards have three basic functions, which illustrate informal and formal approaches to disputes.[41] The ICC Dispute Board Rules explicitly state that once a potential disagreement is perceived, the board may pinpoint the disagreement and urge that parties resolve it on their own without involvement from the board.[42] Alternatively, the board may also settle a dispute by issuing a recommendation or decision "after a procedure of formal referral."[43] All three of these purposes serve an equally important function to reduce risks and costs from disruption to contract performance.

The three kinds of dispute boards are the DAB, the Dispute Review Board ("DRB"), and the Combined Dispute Board ("CDB").[44] A DAB will issue a decision to be complied with immediately.[45] In comparison with DRB, a recommendation will be issued, which is not immediately binding on parties; however, if no party objects within 30 days, then the recommendation will become binding.[46] Lastly, CDBs will provide a solution that falls in the middle of the two. CDBs will usually issue a recommendation but can also issue a decision if one party requests and there is no objection from another party, or if the board decides to do so according to the criteria set forth in the ICC Dispute Board Rules.[47]

3. OVERVIEW OF MAIN INSTITUTIONS AND INSTRUMENTS THAT PLAY A ROLE

It is helpful to understand the fundamental divergence of international arbitration, as well as corresponding institutions and foundational instruments that play a role in developing and harmonizing internationally accepted legal frameworks for recognizing and enforcing arbitral awards and developing

---

[39] *See generally* Bates & Torres-Fowler, *supra* note 27, at 237–64.
[40] *Dispute Boards - ICC - International Chamber of Commerce*, INTERNATIONAL CHAMBER OF COMMERCE (Apr. 3, 2023), https://iccwbo.org/dispute-resolution/dispute-resolution-services/adr/dispute-boards/.
[41] *Id.*
[42] *Id.*
[43] *Id.*
[44] *Id.*
[45] ICC, Dispute Board Rules, Article 5: Dispute Adjudication Boards (DABs).
[46] ICC, Dispute Board Rules, Article 4: Dispute Review Boards (DRBs).
[47] ICC, Dispute Board Rules, Article 6: Combined Dispute Boards (CDBs).

internationally recognized rules for dispute boards. The main institutions and instruments that play prominent roles in offering such services are UNCITRAL, the ICC, FIDIC, and the New York Convention. Additionally, it is important to understand that, in the field of international arbitration, a growing divergence exists between investment and commercial arbitration. This distinction and the key institutional players are briefly highlighted below.

A. A Comparison: Investment Arbitration vs. Commercial Arbitration

International arbitration is a mechanism that produces final and binding determinations of disputes concerning international contracts or other international relationships by independent and impartial arbitrators according to the procedures, structures, and substantive legal standards selected by the consenting parties.[48] This mechanism established confidence in parties to conduct international transactions despite their differing legal, cultural, political, and geographical situations, which are often the source of disagreement among contracting parties.[49] Such differences influence the interpretation of contract terms, the legal implications that stem from a contract, and those parties' respective rights and obligations.[50]

Foreign investments are integral in developing the world economy. Developing countries will engage in major infrastructure projects through foreign investments which, in turn, have significant influence on those countries' economies.[51] This makes the foreign investments vulnerable to interference by the host state.[52] States enter bilateral and multilateral treaties to foster trust and protect the citizens involved. Some countries also enact investment laws to provide legal certainty and encourage further foreign investment.[53] Since investors fear losing their money, they tend to have little faith in obtaining unbiased resolutions through state courts should issues arise.[54] Meanwhile, states are also unwilling to submit disputes to foreign courts.[55] For these reasons, arbitration plays a

---

[48] Julian D.M. Lew, Stefan Kröll, Loukas A. Mistelis, et al., *Chapter 1 Arbitration as a Dispute Settlement Mechanism,* in COMPARATIVE INTERNATIONAL COMMERCIAL ARBITRATION 1 (The Hague: Kluwer Law International, 2003).
[49] *Id.*
[50] *Id.*
[51] Julian D.M. Lew, Stefan Kröll, Loukas A. Mistelis, et al., *Chapter 28 Arbitration of Investment Disputes*, in COMPARATIVE INTERNATIONAL COMMERCIAL ARBITRATION 761–62 (The Hague: Kluwer Law International, 2003).
[52] *Id.*
[53] *Id.*
[54] *Id.*
[55] *Id.*

prominent role when resolving investment disputes.

The central difference between commercial arbitration and investment arbitration is the source of the arbitral tribunal's power: commercial arbitration requires an agreement between parties, whereas investment arbitration is possible without such an agreement.[56] With investment arbitration, treaties or national legislation can empower parties with the right to initiate arbitration proceedings without any contractual relationship at all.[57] This characteristic led to categorizing investment arbitration as "arbitration without privity"[58] of contract. States will agree to provisions in international treaties or national investment protection laws, which then create unilateral standing for the public to pursue arbitration against any party that fulfills the requirements of those provisions.[59] The tribunal then interprets any statutes, treaties, or conventions to determine whether the state is obligated to arbitrate that investment dispute in question.[60] Special purpose companies, their shareholders, or other investors down the line of control facilitating development often make investments.[61]

Arbitrations that involve "investments by parties from one country in another and disputes concerning energy-related issues"[62] both possess issues characteristic of international law. The parties and contracts involved distinguish which type of arbitration is qualified to resolve those disputes. State participation or state sovereignty implications characterize public international arbitrations, and thus, they are subject to certain rules.[63] More specifically, investment arbitrations take place within "the broader framework of public international treaty interpretation," where state conduct is scrutinized based on whether it fulfilled its treaty obligations.[64] For this reason, investment arbitrations are distinct from the contractually based commercial arbitrations that typically exist between private parties.

For commercial arbitration, the parties express their consent to arbitrate

---

[56] *Id.* at 764.
[57] *Id.*
[58] *Id.*
[59] *Id.* at 765.
[60] *Id.*
[61] *Id.*
[62] Julian D.M. Lew, Stefan Kröll, Loukas A. Mistelis, et al., *Chapter 4 Essential Characteristics of International Commercial Arbitration,* in COMPARATIVE INTERNATIONAL COMMERCIAL ARBITRATION 50 (The Hague: Kluwer Law International, 2003).
[63] *Id.*
[64] Tamar Meshel, *Procedural Cross-Fertilization in International Commercial and Investment Arbitration: A Functional Approach*, 12 J. INT'L DISPUTE SETTLEMENT 585–616 (Dec. 2021).

through an arbitration agreement, as the clause in a contract designates.[65] Within the realm of international arbitration, "any international arbitration between companies where the dispute is economic in character" should be considered commercial.[66] This approach is universally accepted and found in the UNCITRAL Model Law on international commercial arbitration.[67] Permanent arbitral institutions like those mentioned later in this article are set up around the world to handle the majority of international commercial arbitrations.[68] Heightened efficiency stems from the existence of these institutions and the application of their procedural rules. However, parties must mutually intend to submit their disputes to that institution for these institutions to have jurisdiction.

B. UNCITRAL

The UNCITRAL promotes the development of legal framework to facilitate international trade and investment across borders.[69] The UNCITRAL mandate is to "further the progressive harmonization and modernization of the law of international trade,"[70] and it plays a key role in such development by promoting and preparing legislative and non-legislative instruments in commercial law. The legal texts develop through a collaborative international process, where various UNCITRAL members represent their respective legal traditions and differing economic status, and the procedure cultivates UNCITRAL texts that are then widely accepted as solutions for numerous countries with varying stages of economic development.[71] Founded in 1966 by the United Nations ("UN") General Assembly, UNCITRAL is comprised of sixty Member States. Its establishment was an outcome of apparent "obstacles to the flow of trade"[72] due to disparities in national laws that governed trade. As a result, the UN sought to remove those obstacles and over time UNCITRAL has formulated "modern, fair, and harmonized rules"[73] for commercial transactions.

---

[65] *Id.* at 593–94.
[66] Philippe Fouchard, Emmanuel Gaillard, and Berthold Goldman, *Part 1: Chapter I - Definition of International Commercial Arbitration*, in FOUCHARD, GAILLARD, GOLDMAN ON INTERNATIONAL COMMERCIAL ARBITRATION, 35 (ed. John Savage, The Hague: Kluwer Law International, 1999).
[67] *Id.*
[68] *Id.* at 33.
[69] *United Nations Commission on International Trade Law*, UNITED NATIONS, https://uncitral.un.org (last visited July 16, 2023).
[70] *Id.*
[71] *Id.*
[72] *About UNCITRAL*, UNCITRAL, https://uncitral.un.org/en/about (last visited Apr. 19, 2024).
[73] *Texts and Status*, UNCITRAL, https://uncitral.un.org/en/texts (last visited Apr.

In lieu of litigation, UNCITRAL is a main promoter of alternative dispute resolution ("ADR"), which is known to be the most traditional dispute resolution method. Litigation, in addition to being expensive and subject to public scrutiny, has limitations with regard to its effect on international disputes; unless bilateral or multilateral treaties are enforced, judgments rendered through state courts are only enforceable within that nation where litigation occurred.[74] In favor of ADR, UNCITRAL has facilitated its adoption through Model laws, such as the UNCITRAL Model Law on International Commercial Arbitration ("Model Law on Arbitration")[75] and the UNCITRAL Model Law on International Commercial Mediation and International Settlement Agreements Resulting from Mediation ("Model Law on Mediation").[76] There has been continued discussion about developing an additional UNCITRAL Model Law on International Commercial Adjudication designed to benefit the international construction industry.

At present, the range of ADR methods falls within the following two distinct categories: consensual and imposed resolutions. Consensual resolutions are facilitated through the Model Law on Mediation, and imposed resolutions are facilitated through the Model Law on Arbitration.[77] In 2018, UNCITRAL stated that "adjudication would facilitate use of a particular tool that had demonstrated its utility in efficiently resolving disputes in a specific sector,"[78] and suggested that the international construction industry could benefit from an additional dispute resolution process, namely a new Model Law for adjudication. UNCITRAL recognized the need for "urgent resolution of disputes through summary proceedings,"[79] particularly "with respect to the enforcement of the

---

19, 2024).

[74] *See Texts and Status: International Commercial Arbitration*, UNCITRAL, https://uncitral.un.org/en/texts/arbitration (last visited Mar. 7, 2024); *see also Texts and Status: International Commercial Mediation*, UNCITRAL, https://uncitral.un.org/en/texts/mediation (last visited Mar. 7, 2024).

[75] *UNCITRAL Model Law on International Commercial Mediation and International Settlement Agreements Resulting from Mediation, 2018*, UNCITRAL, https://uncitral.un.org/en/texts/mediation/modellaw/commercial_conciliation (last visited July 16, 2023).

[76] *Id.*

[77] *See Texts and Status: International Commercial Arbitration*, UNCITRAL, https://uncitral.un.org/en/texts/arbitration (last visited Mar. 7, 2024); *see also Texts and Status: International Commercial Mediation*, UNCITRAL, https://uncitral.un.org/en/texts/mediation (last visited Mar. 7, 2024).

[78] United Nations General Assembly, *Report of the United Nations Commission on International Trade Law*, ¶ 245, U.N. Doc. A/73/17, July 31, 2018, United Nations Commission on International Trade Law.

[79] United Nations General Assembly, *Report of the United Nations Commission*

interim decision by the adjudicator."⁸⁰

C. ICC

The ICC deems itself a "one-stop shop for all dispute resolution and avoidance needs of businesses everywhere."⁸¹ The ICC serves as an institutional representative of companies from over 170 countries and, therefore, serves companies by helping to resolve disputes quickly and efficiently.⁸² It does this by offering effective and timely alternatives to litigation, thereby enabling "access to justice" globally for individuals, private sector enterprises, states, and state entities.⁸³ Based in Paris, France, the ICC's three core activities are rule setting, arbitration, and policy.⁸⁴ Simultaneously, the ICC provides services, including ICC Arbitration, training, and customs facilitation. The organization represents and helps establish rules that "affect and govern the interests of individuals and organizations in every part of private enterprise."⁸⁵ It advocates its policies, establishes rules to assist members in adhering to those policies, and solves disputes between its members.⁸⁶ The ICC is considered the world's biggest business organization aiming to promote international trade and investment, and it exercises great power when developing the rules and policies that govern how to conduct business transactions in the sphere of international business.⁸⁷

The ICC Dispute Board Rules include a "comprehensive set of provisions for establishing and operating"⁸⁸ a dispute board. The ICC advises that parties using

---

on International Trade Law, ¶ 265, U.N. Doc. A/72/17, July 2017, United Nations Commission on International Trade Law.
⁸⁰ *Id.*
⁸¹ *About ICC Dispute Resolution*, INTERNATIONAL CHAMBER OF COMMERCE, https://iccwbo.org/dispute-resolution/about-icc-dispute-resolution-services/ (last visited July 14, 2023).
⁸² *Id.*
⁸³ *International Chamber of Commerce*, ICC (June 28, 2023), https://iccwbo.org/, (last visited July 14, 2023).
⁸⁴ *International Chamber of Commerce (ICC)*, USCIB (June 27, 2022), https://uscib.org/international-chamber-of-commerce-icc-ud-754/.
⁸⁵ *See International Chamber of Commerce (ICC)*, CORPORATE FINANCE INSTITUTE (Jan. 19, 2023), https://corporatefinanceinstitute.com/resources/economics/international-chamber-of-commerce-icc/.
⁸⁶ *Id.*
⁸⁷ *Id.*
⁸⁸ *See Dispute Boards*, INTERNATIONAL CHAMBER OF COMMERCE (Apr. 3, 2023), https://iccwbo.org/dispute-resolution/dispute-resolution-services/adr/dispute-boards/.

these rules should "include an appropriate clause in their contract"[89] depending on which of the three types of dispute boards they wish to use. Each type of board is distinguishable by the conclusion that it issues once parties follow the procedure of a formal referral to the board. For this reason, the ICC provides standard ICC Dispute Board Clauses for each board type. The ICC also suggests a model Dispute Board Member Agreement to address matters such as the board member's "undertaking and remuneration, as well as the duration of the agreement."[90]

The ICC Dispute Resolution Statistics revealed that there was a shocking increase in the number of newly registered cases in 2020, many of which were small disputes.[91] There was also a record-breaking number of new cases registered that year under the "ICC Rules of Mediation, Expert Rules and DOCDEX Rules."[92] The ICC established Expedited Procedure Provisions ("EPP") to achieve proportionate resolutions that match "the increasing number of cases with an amount in dispute not exceeding"[93] two million United States ("US") Dollars ("USD").[94]

D. The New York Convention

A 2018 survey titled "International Arbitration Survey: The Evolution of International Arbitration" by White & Case and Queen Mary University of London revealed that "the two most valuable characteristics of international arbitration are enforceability of awards and avoiding specific legal systems"[95] or national courts. These characteristics stem from The Convention on the Recognition and Enforcement of Foreign Arbitral Awards, also known as the New York Convention[96] ("the Convention"). The Convention is recognized as "the most successful multilateral instrument in the field of international trade law"[97] and serves as the "touchstone" for international commercial arbitration. Its primary objective is to provide "common legislative standards for the recognition

---

[89] *Id.*
[90] *Id.*
[91] *See* ICC DISPUTE RESOLUTION STATISTICS: 2020, INTERNATIONAL CHAMBER OF COMMERCE 12 (2021), https://iccwbo.org/news-publications/arbitration-adr-rules-and-tools/icc-dispute-resolution-statistics-2020/.
[92] *Id.*
[93] *Id.*
[94] *Id.* at 14.
[95] *See* O'Malley, *supra* note 24, at 51.
[96] *See* Convention on the Recognition and Enforcement of Foreign Arbitral Awards, UNCITRAL (1958), https://uncitral.un.org/sites/uncitral.un.org/files/media-documents/uncitral/en/new-york-convention-e.pdf (last visited Mar. 7, 2024).
[97] *See* O'Malley, *supra* note 24, at 52.

of arbitration agreements and court recognition and enforcement of foreign and non-domestic arbitral awards."[98]

In addition to the 171 parties to the Convention,[99] the Convention achieved this objective since recognition and enforcement also apply to all foreign awards, including those made outside treaty countries. The goal was to prevent foreign and non-domestic arbitral awards from discrimination and to obligate Parties to guarantee recognition of the awards so that enforcement in their jurisdiction is feasible in the same manner as domestic awards.[100] Another goal was to require national courts of Parties to honor arbitration agreements by referring the matters to an arbitral tribunal and thus denying access to court in an effort not to contravene the agreement.[101]

The main obligation imposed on Parties is "to recognize all arbitral awards … as binding and enforce them, if requested to do so, under the lex fori,"[102] with five defined grounds for which such recognition and enforcement can be refused. Those grounds include due process, incapacity of the parties, invalidity of the arbitration agreement, scope of the arbitration agreement, and jurisdiction of the arbitral tribunal, otherwise suspending or setting aside the award in the country, or under the law of, which the award was made.[103]

E. FIDIC

FIDIC contracts have growing utilization in renewable energy projects, particularly in the wind farm subsector encompassing both onshore and offshore ventures. When it comes to offshore wind projects, substantial modifications were made to FIDIC forms to address the specific requirements of such projects.[104] Therefore, it is imperative to develop a balanced FIDIC contract tailored to the

---

[98] *See* Convention on the Recognition and Enforcement of Foreign Arbitral Awards, *supra* note 96.

[99] Suriname became the 171st State Party to the Convention, which entered into force for Suriname on 8 February 2023. *Suriname accedes to Convention on the Recognition and Enforcement of Foreign Arbitral Awards*, UN INFO. SERVS. VIENNA (Nov. 23, 2022), https://unis.unvienna.org/unis/en/pressrels/2022/unisl334.html.

[100] Convention on the Recognition and Enforcement of Foreign Arbitral Awards, *supra* note 96, at 1.

[101] *Id.*

[102] *Id.* at 2.

[103] *Id.*

[104] David Foxwell, *FIDIC Begins Work on New Contract Intended Specifically for Offshore Wind Projects*, RIVIERA (July 6, 2023), https://www.rivieramm.com/news-content-hub/news-content-hub/work-starts-on-new-fidic-contract-for-offshore-wind-projects-76836.

offshore wind sector's requirements and special features.

In the last 100 years, consulting engineers have had a substantial influence on global society, with groundbreaking progress and innovative advances in "transport, water supply, energy, buildings, and vital infrastructure"[105] which resulted in enhanced health, economic growth, and ultimately, a significant improvement in the standard of living. Nevertheless, a considerable portion of humanity continues to face challenges related to access to food, clean water, and basic survival. It is imperative to tackle these issues more effectively. Merely relying on technical solutions is inadequate when it comes to the broader conversations surrounding "efficient governance and restricted finance."[106]

Founded in 1913, the FIDIC is an organization that establishes international standards related to construction technology and consulting engineering.[107] Throughout the 1990s, the Federation gradually grew to the global level, representing regions all over the world. FIDIC now plays an essential role in the consulting engineering industry,[108] serving as the industry's voice on a global level.

Now the international standard, FIDIC Contracts are recognized and utilized in numerous jurisdictions and for a variety of project types. The key factor that contributed to their achievement as an industry standard is their "balanced approach to the roles and responsibilities of the main parties"[109] involved, including risk management and allocation. Hence, for FIDIC contracts, the underlying fundamental principle is the utilization of "General Conditions of Contract,"[110] which are considered suitable for all situations based on the success of thousands of projects worldwide. However, it is important to recognize that each project is unique, and FIDIC acknowledges the need for special conditions to address project-specific issues on a case-by-case basis.[111] Therefore, all FIDIC contracts include guidance on the creation of "Particular Conditions" and offer examples of such situations where specific provisions may be necessary for a particular project.[112] Deviating significantly from these guidelines increases the risk of disturbing the balanced nature of the contract and jeopardizing the successful execution of the project. Research and experience from different clients

---

[105] *History*, FIDIC, https://fidic.org/history (last visited July 14, 2023).
[106] *Id.*
[107] *Id.*
[108] *Id.*
[109] *Why Use FIDIC Contracts?*, FIDIC, https://fidic.org/node/7089 (last visited July 14, 2023).
[110] *Id.*
[111] *Id.*
[112] *Id.*

and countries indicate that an upset in the risk-sharing balance in FIDIC contracts usually leads to: "higher tender prices; delays to completion; additional time and cost claims;"[113] and, in severe cases, prolonged disputes resulting in arbitration or contract termination.

The FIDIC makes project-specific sub-clauses available for guidance where "Particular Conditions" may be used.[114] However, drafters should note that there are non-project specific clauses that are thought never to be modified.[115]

i. Overview of FIDIC Legal Frameworks

Dispute boards grew in popularity over their fifty-plus years of existence, particularly with large-scale international construction contracts. A massive number of "standard form construction agreements [...] have included dispute boards as condition precedents to formal arbitration,"[116] and the standard form FIDIC agreements are arguably the most popular. These standard form agreements are the trusted international industry standards found in the FIDIC Suite of Contracts (known as "Books") as templates classified by their color and organized based on the "extent of design and other responsibilities assumed by the Employer and the Contractor."[117] In 1999, FIDIC made a historical revision to its various forms of contract by introducing a dispute adjudication board as a principal means to resolve disputes.[118] These revisions were seen in the FIDIC "Red Book" and the FIDIC "Yellow Book," which are the two best-known publications of standard forms of contracts.[119] Standard form FIDIC contracts are suitable for parties from different nationalities and jurisdictions.

The Red Book, "Conditions of Contract for Construction," is the standard construction contract form for projects where the employer does the design of

---

[113] *Id.*

[114] *Id.*

[115] A list of non-project specific clauses that are thought to never be modified are available at FIDIC's website, https://fidic.org/node/7089.

[116] *See* Bates & Torres-Fowler, *supra* note 27, at 238.

[117] *See The FIDIC Suite of Contracts*, FIDIC, https://fidic.org/sites/default/files/FIDIC_Suite_of_Contracts_0.pdf (last visited Apr. 19, 2024).

[118] *See* P. H. J. Chapman et al, *Dispute Boards on Major Infrastructure Projects*, PROCEEDINGS OF THE INSTITUTION OF CIVIL ENGINEERS - MANAGEMENT, PROCUREMENT AND LAW (ICE Publishing, May 25, 2015), https://www.icevirtuallibrary.com/doi/10.1680/mpal.2009.162.1.7 (last visited July 12, 2023).

[119] *See The FIDIC Suite of Contracts*, FIDIC, https://fidic.org/sites/default/files/FIDIC_Suite_of_Contracts_0.pdf (last visited Apr. 19, 2024).

building and engineering works.[120] The Engineer, that is employed by the Employer, does the Project's administration and supervision; that Engineer is responsible for issuing instructions, certifying payments, as well as determining completion,[121] so the Red Book is suitable when works are designed predominantly by the Employer.[122] The contractor is normally paid on a measurement basis for quantities of work actually performed, using the prices and rates per the bill of quantities (although there is the option to be paid a lump sum).[123]

The Yellow Book, "Conditions of Contract for Plant and Design Build," is a standard contract for projects where the design (M&E, building, and engineering works) is done by the contractor.[124] The Engineer, hired by the Employer, administers and supervises the project and is responsible for issuing instructions, certifying payments, and determining completion.[125] The Contractor usually provides and designs the works according to the Employers requirements, including "any combination of civil, mechanical, electrical and/or construction works"; so, when the work is designed predominantly by the contractor, the Yellow Book is suitable.[126] The contractor is normally paid interim payments of a lump sum, typically in installments as specified in the payment schedule.[127]

Both the Yellow and Red Books provide a procedure for resolving disputes.[128] When disputes arise, the supervising Engineer is required to consult each party in an attempt to reach an agreement, and if an agreement cannot be made, then the engineer makes a "fair determination" considering all relevant circumstances to the dispute.[129] If either party disagrees with that determination, the issue is referred to the dispute adjudication board.[130] That dispute adjudication board consists of one or three jointly appointed people by the parties.[131] If either party refuses to accept the dispute board's decision, the final determination will

---

[120] *Id.*
[121] *Id.*
[122] *Id.*
[123] *Id.*
[124] *Id.*
[125] *Id.*
[126] *Id.*
[127] *Id.*
[128] *See The FIDIC Suite of Contracts*, FIDIC, https://fidic.org/sites/default/files/FIDIC_Suite_of_Contracts_0.pdf (last visited Apr. 19, 2024).
[129] *Id.*
[130] *Id.*
[131] *Id.*

be made through international arbitration.[132]

4. LEGAL ASPECTS OF DISPUTE BOARDS

A. How Do Dispute Boards Work?

In general, the commencement of a contract leads to the creation of dispute boards, which are bodies of members, usually one or three.[133] These boards function to assist parties in avoiding, overcoming, or resolving any disputes that may appear while the contract is implemented.[134] While dispute boards are used in many sectors, they are common in the pursuance of construction projects.[135] For this reason, the use of dispute boards would be sensible for future contracting parties to renewable energy projects.

The basic functions of dispute boards are to reduce risks and costs of potential disruptions to the parties' contracts.[136] This is done by encouraging parties to resolve issues amongst themselves, or where disputes may be more complex, the board may intervene through informal or formal approaches to resolve the issue prior to arbitration.[137] A board may intervene informally to assist parties in agreeing to a resolution.[138] Otherwise, the board decides either by issuing a recommendation or a decision once the dispute is formally referred to the board.[139]

The latest edition of the FIDIC Red Book emphasizes dispute avoidance rather than mere dispute decision-making. Consequently, the FIDIC makes a strong recommendation to appoint a standing board[140] to assist parties on a continuous basis to both avoid and decide disputes when necessary. This is because only a permanently available standing board can perform the Dispute avoidance function.[141]

---

[132] *Id.*
[133] *See Dispute Boards*, INTERNATIONAL CHAMBER OF COMMERCE, Dispute Resolution Services, ADR (Apr. 3, 2023), https://iccwbo.org/dispute-resolution/dispute-resolution-services/adr/dispute-boards/.
[134] *Id.*
[135] *See Dispute Boards, supra* note 133.
[136] *Id.*
[137] *Id.*
[138] *Id.*
[139] *Id.*
[140] *See* FIDIC, CONDITIONS OF CONTRACT FOR CONSTRUCTION § 21.1 (2017) [hereinafter "RED BOOK"].
[141] *See* Christopher Seppälä, *Chapter IV: Clause-by-Clause Commentary*, in THE FIDIC RED BOOK CONTRACT: AN INTERNATIONAL CLAUSE-BY-CLAUSE COMMENTARY 1207 (Alphen aan den Rijn: Kluwer Law International, 2023).

B. Different Forms of Boards: Standing vs. Ad Hoc

i. *Standing*

A standing board is appointed at the start of a contract and remains or "stands" in place for the duration of the contract.[142] Standing dispute boards are the preferred board form for long-term business relationships, since it is required to remain familiar with the project's details, to visit the project site regularly, and to assist Parties with dispute resolution.[143]

ii. *Ad Hoc*

Compared to standing boards, *ad hoc* boards can be appropriate for many other circumstances. Particularly, a formalized *ad hoc* dispute board process can be used as a substitution for mediation.[144] An *ad hoc* dispute adjudication board is appointed only when a dispute arises; then that board renders a decision for that dispute, and the board is terminated when the decision is rendered.[145]

C. Rules of Procedure: Examination of the Governing Rules and Guidelines

Since its original development in 1957, the FIDIC Suite of Contracts has provided professionals with project guidelines and governing rules of procedure.[146] In 1999, FIDIC published a revised suite of contracts, including updated versions of the Red and Yellow books, to adjust for industry developments and to more effectively prepare for dispute resolution by including dispute adjudication boards.[147] The second edition of the Red Book was updated in 2017, amending the Disputes and Arbitration Clause (Clause 21) "dealing with the procedure for settling disputes and arbitration, whereas in [the 1999 Red Book] these were dealt with in Sub-Clauses 20.2 to 20.8."[148] The following procedural rules reflect the core governing rules for dispute boards in the 1999

---

[142] The new "Disputes and Arbitration" clause in the FIDIC Red Book (Clause 21) provides for the constitution of a standing board. RED BOOK § 21.1.
[143] *Id.*
[144] *See generally* Bates & Torres-Fowler, *supra* note 27, at 237–64.
[145] *See The FIDIC Suite of Contracts*, FIDIC, https://fidic.org/sites/default/files/FIDIC_Suite_of_Contracts_0.pdf (last visited Apr. 19, 2024).
[146] *Id.*
[147] *Id.*
[148] *See* Christopher Seppälä, *Chapter IV: Clause-by-Clause Commentary*, in THE FIDIC RED BOOK CONTRACT: AN INTERNATIONAL CLAUSE-BY-CLAUSE COMMENTARY 1200 (Alphen aan den Rijn: Kluwer Law International, 2023) [hereinafter *Chapter IV*].

Red [and Yellow] book[s] while indicating amendments to the latest edition of the 2017 Red Book since the Red Book is "the most widely used standard form of international construction contracts."[149] It is important to note the slight change in terminology; the DAB is now referred to as the Dispute Avoidance/Adjudication Board ("DAAB").[150]

The Red Book offers a widely used standard contract in international construction or civil engineering projects.[151] The contract essentially involves three (3) parties: "the owner or employer, the contractor, and the engineer."[152] To understand the procedural aspects discussed below, it is important to note that the "Engineer" is generally a firm of consultants, engineers, or architects acting on behalf of the owner "under a separate contract to assist the owner [...] during the performance of the works" of the project.[153] The FIDIC Conditions provide detailed procedures to resolve disputes that arise between the parties, either by the Engineer or thereafter, through the DAAB or arbitration.

D. Constituting the Dispute Board

The composition of a dispute board is the selection and qualification of board members, and appointment includes appointing dispute board members who establish the dispute board. According to the Red Book, a DAAB shall decide disputes in accordance with Sub-Clause 21.4, "Obtaining DAAB's Decision".[154] When constituting a dispute board, the contract Clause will name the jointly appointed member(s) of the DAAB within a time frame stated in the Contract Data, or if no time frame is stated, within twenty-eight (28) days following the day the Contractor received the Letter of Acceptance.[155] A DAAB shall comprise either one qualified member (the "sole member") or three qualified members ("members").[156] If the quantity of appointed members is not specified, the DAAB

---

[149] *See* Christopher Seppälä, *Chapter I: General Introduction*, in THE FIDIC RED BOOK CONTRACT: AN INTERNATIONAL CLAUSE-BY-CLAUSE COMMENTARY 1 (Alphen aan den Rijn: Kluwer Law International, 2023).
[150] *See Chapter IV, supra* note 148, at 1230.
[151] *See* Philippe Fouchard, Emmanuel Gaillard, and Berthold Goldman, *Part 1: Chapter I - Definition of International Commercial Arbitration*, in FOUCHARD, GAILLARD, GOLDMAN ON INTERNATIONAL COMMERCIAL ARBITRATION 17 (John Savage ed., The Hague: Kluwer Law International, 1999).
[152] *Id.*
[153] *Id.*
[154] *See* RED BOOK § 21.4.
[155] The 1999 Red Book merely provided for appointment of the DAB "by the date stated in the Appendix to Tender." FIDIC, CONDITIONS OF CONTRACT FOR CONSTRUCTION § 20.2 (1999).
[156] *See* RED BOOK § 21.1.

will comprise of three members.[157]

The board members (either the sole member or three members) are selected from a named list in the Contract Data[158] and must be willing and able to accept the appointment. When a board is comprised of three members, each Party selects one member for the agreement[159] of the other Party, and they must also consult both of those members to then agree on the third member to act as chairperson. The board is officially constituted on the day Parties and DAAB member(s) all sign a DAAB agreement.[160] Any replacement of a suitably qualified person is appointed in the same original manner, and unless parties agree otherwise, a replacement DAAB member is appointed if a member declines to act or is unable to act.[161] Any member's appointment may be terminated through a mutual agreement of the Parties. However, this is not permitted by either the Employer or the Contractor acting alone.

Unless otherwise agreed, the term and appointment of each member of the DAAB expires either on the specified date of discharge or twenty-eight (28) days after all disputed decisions are given, whichever is later.[162] However, when a contract is terminated earlier according to any sub-clauses of the stated conditions, the DAAB's term expires twenty-eight (28) days after either the DAAB gave decisions on all disputes referred to it within two-hundred-twenty-four (224) days after the date of termination; or the date that Parties finally agree on all matters regarding termination, including payment, whichever is earlier (between the decision or the final agreement).[163]

E. Decision-making Process: Evaluation of the Process Followed by Dispute Boards in Reaching Decisions

Sub-Clause 3.7 provides a procedure that allows the Engineer to assist the parties in resolving any matter relating to the main contract or execution of the project.[164] The clause requires that, for any matter referred to the Engineer, the Engineer must give a determination or it must otherwise be resolved through

---

[157] *Id.*
[158] *Compare* FIDIC, CONDITIONS OF CONTRACT FOR CONSTRUCTION § 20.2 (1999), which instructed DAB members to be selected from a list as an option.
[159] *Compare id.*, which stated each Party was to nominate a member for the "approval" of the other party.
[160] *See* RED BOOK § 21.1.
[161] *See id.* (a member is considered "unable to act" due to death, illness, disability, resignation or termination of appointment).
[162] *Id.*
[163] *Id.*
[164] *See id.* § 3.7.

agreement between the parties.[165] Any dissatisfied party must give notice of its dissatisfaction ("NOD") with the determination within twenty-eight (28) if it wishes to pursue the issue further—thereby creating a "Dispute" as defined in Sub-Clause 1.1.29.[166] Thereafter, the parties may refer the dispute to the DAAB for a decision.

Since the change in the Red Book provisions, a noteworthy difference is that the 2017 Red Book places greater emphasis on the duty of the DAAB to assist in avoiding disputes rather than just deciding them. The FIDIC states:

> Construction projects depend for their success on *the avoidance of Disputes* [...] and, if disputes arise [their timely resolution].
>
> Therefore, the Contract should include [...] Clause 21 which, while not discouraging the Parties from reaching their own agreement on Disputes as the Works proceed, allow them to bring contentious matters to an independent and impartial dispute avoidance/adjudication board (DAAB) for resolution.[167]

As mentioned earlier, a standing board is strongly recommended to facilitate the Dispute Avoidance function. Clause 21 of the 2017 Red Book outlines the DAAB's two functions: Dispute Avoidance and Dispute Resolution.[168] Put simply, the Dispute Avoidance[169] function has no detailed time limit or special procedure. Parties may jointly refer any disagreement or issue to the DAAB, and the DAAB then provides informal assistance to attempt to resolve that disagreement or issue.[170] Pursuant to Sub-Clause 21.3, Parties may not jointly request assistance from the DAAB when the Engineer is considering the issue in accordance with Sub-Clause 3.7 to allow the Engineer to perform his or her function to resolve the matter.[171] Additionally, the DAAB may invite Parties to make a referral if the DAAB becomes aware of any issues. Both parties must be present at the discussions, but any advice given by the DAAB is not binding to

---

[165] *Id.*

[166] *See id.* § 1.1.29.

[167] Before DABs were introduced to the Red Book in 1999, the Engineer decided disputes prior to arbitration. *See* RED BOOK § 21.1.

[168] *Id.*

[169] *See id.* § 21.3.

[170] This feature is distinct from the 1999 Red Book since the 1999 version merely provided Parties *could* jointly refer issues to the DAB for an opinion if the Parties so agreed.

[171] *Id.*

either party nor the DAAB if a decision is requested later on.

In contrast to dispute avoidance, the Dispute Resolution[172] function does have strict time limits and procedures. The parties formally refer a dispute to the DAAB, and the DAAB then issues a decision. If the decision does not resolve the dispute, parties then attempt to reach an amicable settlement pursuant to Sub-Clause 21.5.[173] If the parties cannot reach an amicable settlement, then a final resolution will be sought through arbitration by the ICC pursuant to Sub-Clause 21.6.[174]

Regardless of whether the parties sought informal discussions through dispute avoidance, either party may refer a dispute to the DAAB for a decision when a dispute arises. In addition to Sub-Clause 1.1.29 defining Dispute, the Red Book deems a dispute to have arisen if:

> (a) there is a failure as referred to under sub-paragraph (b), or a non-payment as referred to under sub-paragraph (c), of Sub-Clause 16.2.1 [*Notice*];
>
> (b) the Contractor is entitled to receive financing charges under Sub-Clause 14.8 [*Delayed Payment*] but does not receive payment thereof from the Employer within 28 days after his request for such payments; or
>
> (c) a Party has given:
>
> (i) a Notice of intention to terminate the Contract under Sub-Clause 15.2.1 [*Notice*] or Sub-Clause 16.2.1 [*Notice*] (as the case may be); or
> (ii) a Notice of termination under Sub-Clause 15.2.2 [*Termination*], Sub-Clause 16.2.2 [*Termination*], 18.5 [*Optional Termination*] or Sub-Clause 18.6 [*Release from Performance under the Law*] (as the case may be);
> and the other Party has disagreed with the first Party's entitlement to give such Notice.[175]

Either Party may then refer a dispute under Sub-Clause 21.4 without the need

---

[172] *See id.* § 21.4.
[173] *See id.* § 21.5.
[174] *See id.* §§ 21.5–6.
[175] *See id.* §§ 15.2.1, 16.2.1.

for a notice of dissatisfaction.[176] Generally speaking though, Sub-Clause 3.7.5 requires that a NOD with an engineer's determination first be either given or received. Parties then have forty-five (45) days to refer a dispute to the DAAB.[177] If the Parties do not refer the dispute within that time window, the NOD is deemed invalid. After formal reference to the board, parties must make all information available to the DAAB, including access to the project site and its facilities. The DAAB has eighty-four (84) days from the date of receipt of reference to give its decision unless otherwise agreed by the parties or within whatever period was proposed by the board.[178] The DAAB is permitted to withhold its decision until all outstanding or overdue invoices are fully paid.[179]

F. Where a Dispute Board Decision is a Condition Precedent to Arbitration

The only matters Parties are permitted to submit to arbitration are those Disputes that were formally referred to the DAAB for a decision and not subject to the decision as final and binding because a party gave adequate notice of its dissatisfaction with that decision within twenty-eight (28) days.[180] Sub-Clause 21.2, first sentence, states, "Disputes shall be decided by a DAAB," which is the first indication it is mandatory for disputes to be referred to the DAAB for a decision.[181] Sub-Clause 21.4.4 confirms that the dispute board decision is a condition precedent, providing that with exceptions, "neither Party shall be entitled to commence arbitration of a Dispute unless a NOD [with the DAAB's decision] in respect of that Dispute has been given."[182]

Sub-Clause 21.6, first sentence, also states that "[u]nless settled amicably, […], any Dispute in respect of which the DAAB's decision (if any) has not become final and binding shall be finally settled by international arbitration [...]", the 'if any' reference indicating when the DAAB fails to render a decision.[183] There are only some clear exceptions to the condition precedent to arbitration listed under Sub-Clause 21.6 Arbitration. The requirement of prior referral to the DAAB as a condition to arbitration applies to matters or Claims of either Party that give rise to disputes.[184] This means that even when one Party refers a dispute to arbitration, the other Party is not relieved from its obligation to satisfy this requirement for

---

[176] *See id.* § 21.4.
[177] *See id.* § 3.7.5.
[178] *See id.* § 21.4.
[179] *Id.*
[180] *Id.*
[181] *See id.* § 21.1–2.
[182] *See id.* § 21.4.
[183] *See id.* § 21.4.4.
[184] *See id.*

any matters it may pursue; thus, even if the supervising Engineer rejected that other Party's claim and it gave a notice of dissatisfaction, it would still be required to refer the claim as a Dispute to the DAAB prior to arbitration. More simply, once a contractor properly initiates arbitration, if an employer then wants to assert a counterclaim that had not been previously referred to the DAB, the counterclaim will likely be found inadmissible in the proceeding. In the last example, the counterclaim may be admissible if it falls within the scope of a previously referred dispute to the DAB.

G. Enforcement of a DAAB's Decision[185]

The DAAB must give its decision to both parties in writing and include a copy to the Engineer.[186] The decision must be reasoned, stating that it is given under Sub-Clause 21.4.3.[187] That decision is then binding on the parties. The parties are required to promptly comply with the decision regardless of whether they issued a notice of dissatisfaction with respect to that decision. The Sub-Clause places the Employer responsible for ensuring the Engineer's compliance.[188] Any money requirements stated in the decision are due immediately.[189]

H. Dissatisfaction with DAAB's Decision

Either dissatisfied party may give a notice of dissatisfaction to the other party. The NOD must be within twenty-eight (28) days of receipt of the DAAB's decision.[190] It must state that it is a "Notice of Dissatisfaction with the DAAB's Decision" and provide reasons for dissatisfaction. Copies should be made to both the DAAB and the Engineer.[191] If the DAAB fails to issue a decision within the specified time frame under Sub-Clause 21.4.3, then either party may give another NOD within twenty-eight (28) from the expired time period.[192]

NODs are a critical step in the procedural process since, except for instances "stated in Sub-Clause 3.7.5, 21.7, and 21.8, neither Party may commence arbitration of a Dispute unless a NOD in respect of it has been given under Sub-Clause 21.4.4."[193] Additionally, if no NOD is given within twenty-eight (28) days of a decision, that decision is then final and binding. In the case where a party is

---

[185] *See id.* § 21.4.3.
[186] *Id.*
[187] *Id.*
[188] *Id.*
[189] *Id.*
[190] *Id.*
[191] *Id.*
[192] *Id.*
[193] *See Chapter IV, supra* note 148, at 1230.

only partly dissatisfied with a decision, they must identify that part in a NOD, which is then severed from the remaining decision.[194] That remaining decision is then final and binding.

I. Effectiveness of Decisions

"Indeed, while there are a number of factors at play, statistics suggest that binding dispute board decisions are rarely challenged in subsequent litigation or arbitration."[195]

Informal Dispute Avoidance functions as a "face-saving" process. As mentioned, no advice from the DAAB is binding during dispute avoidance.[196] However, the DAAB may still indicate how an issue would be resolved if the dispute is formally referred to the board for a decision later. By knowing this in advance, parties can reevaluate their positions and, in turn, the issue is more likely to be resolved amicably. This prevents one party from being the winner and the other the loser.

J. Some Criticisms

Dispute boards are not without disadvantages; they can be expensive and mandatory and, consequently, may not be the right mechanism for all contractual relationships or construction projects. There are often many steps of procedure to comply with. The procedures may also be susceptible to gamesmanship,[197] and statistical bias may favor claimants in adjudication and be difficult to achieve fairness. Parties can easily avoid the issued recommendations and decisions by dispute boards. Therefore, the utility of those decisions may be questioned if, ultimately, the losing party is not required to follow those decisions. While the adjudication mechanism by an independent and impartial third party produces a decision within a limited time frame, and while such a decision is immediately enforceable, it is also subject to a challenge either through arbitration or litigation.[198] Further, binding determinations cannot be enforced like arbitration awards would be under the New York Convention, and as a result, dispute boards are criticized as an unnecessary, additional, and costly step to finally receive a binding and enforceable determination.[199]

Additionally, multi-tiered arbitration clauses can present difficulties

---

[194] *Id.* at 1231.
[195] *See* Bates & Torres-Fowler, *supra* note 27, at 241.
[196] *Id.*
[197] *See generally* Bates & Torres-Fowler, *supra* note 27, at 237–64.
[198] *See* United Nations General Assembly, *Settlement of Commercial Disputes, Adjudication, Note by the Secretariat*, ¶ 6, U.N. Doc. A/CN.9/WG.II/WP.225, January 27, 2022, UNCITRAL.
[199] *Id.*

concerning arbitral jurisdiction, particularly where an arbitration clause instructs the claimant to bring his or her claims before a body (e.g. engineers, valuers, or DRB/DABs) prior to bringing the claim to arbitration proceedings. When a claimant brings the claim to arbitration proceedings without properly complying with the clause, the respondents to the arbitration proceedings may often object and claim that the failure to bring it to the board was an obstacle to arbitral jurisdiction. This was the case in *X. Ltd v. Y. S.p.A.*, where the arbitrator ruled that the Claimant's failure to bring the claim before the DAB, which the contract in dispute instructed to do, "did not deprive him of his jurisdiction,"[200] and the Federal Supreme Court upheld the award. In this case, the claim proceeded to arbitration before the DAB was able to complete its procedure since the parties had been very slow to set up the DAB.[201] First, the Court considered whether presentation to the DAB was a binding requirement under the DAB clause, which the Court indeed found to be binding in principle; the Court, however, noted exceptions exist.[202] Under the circumstances, the Court considered whether the arbitrator had jurisdiction. It pointed out two points: first, that a main purpose of the DAB was to allow for "swift resolution of disputes,"[203] which had been compromised since the claimant sent notice of the dispute after the project works were completed; and second, that the contract stipulated the DAB was to provide a decision on the dispute presented to it within eighty-four days, but the DAB had required close to fifteen months to constitute.[204] The Court also noted that applicable contract terms required a "Dispute Adjudication Agreement to be in force with each DAB member and each of the parties"[205] to allow the DAB to be considered "in place."[206] The Court, therefore, ruled no DAB was "in place" at the time the claimant brought the arbitration proceedings.[207]

5. CHARACTERISTIC CONSIDERATIONS OF RENEWABLE ENERGY PROJECTS

Dispute boards are a suitable option due to the distinct characteristics of disputes in the construction industry. In essence, construction projects have

---

[200] *See* Paolo Michele Patocchi, *National Report for Switzerland (2018 through 2023)*, in ICCA INTERNATIONAL HANDBOOK ON COMMERCIAL ARBITRATION, Supplement No. 125, at 67, n. 179 (ed. Lise Bosman, Kluwer Law International, 2023).
[201] *Id.*
[202] *Id.* at 68.
[203] *Id.*
[204] *Id.*
[205] *Id.*
[206] *Id.*
[207] *Id.*

lengthy durations, complex engineering, and numerous claims and disputes to work out. These features set construction contracts apart from most other business relationships. At their core, disputes to international construction projects generally entail claims for breach of contract (e.g., one Party accuses another of failing to meet their end of the bargain). However, the claims raised are nuanced issues compared to other contractual relationships.[208] It is common for construction projects to face hundreds or even thousands of "highly technical engineering disputes" that, on their own, are suitable for individual arbitration.[209] Individually those claims may be considered small, but collectively the claims significantly impact a project's cost and timeline for completion. The long-term nature and nuanced context behind these projects cause reluctance to refer disputes to local courts. Besides avoiding significant costs for litigating each claim, parties fear that foreign national courts lack the expertise and the neutrality to resolve claims properly.

6. LOOKING FORWARD

Arbitration became noticeably more burdensome with unfavorable similarities to litigation. In response to concerns around the lengthier timelines and increasing costs, expedited arbitration procedures were a recent focus of arbitral institutions. A "common international expedited procedure framework" was increasingly demanded to cope with more straightforward arbitration cases, but such international mechanisms were lacking.[210] It was also pointed out that in the context of long-term projects, where work needed to proceed despite any disagreements around quality or payment, adjudication was a useful tool.[211] Adjudication clauses had historical use, and subsequently, many jurisdictions had already enacted legislation on adjudication.[212] In 2018, UNCITRAL reported that model legislative provisions and contractual clauses for adjudication could further facilitate its use and that both expedited arbitration procedure and adjudication fit well together[213] as solutions to expedited dispute resolution. The former provided generally applicable tools to reduce costs and time windows of arbitration, while the latter facilitated using a tool with a demonstrated utility for resolving disputes

---

[208] *See generally*, Jane Jenkins, *Chapter 1 — Introduction, §1.01 What Is Special About International Construction Disputes?*, in INTERNATIONAL CONSTRUCTION ARBITRATION LAW (2d. ed., Kluwer Law International, 2014).
[209] Bates & Torres-Fowler, *supra* note 27, at 239.
[210] United Nations General Assembly, *Report of Working Group II (Dispute Settlement) on the work of its sixty-eighth session (New York, 5-9 February 2018)*, ¶ 153, U.N. Doc. A/CN.9/934, January 19, 2018, UNCITRAL.
[211] *Id.* ¶ 154.
[212] *Id.*
[213] *Id.* ¶ 155.

efficiently in a specific sector. While the success of adjudication as a tool was renowned specifically in the international construction sector,[214] it is believed that the development of an internationally recognized framework would pave the way for its adoption and broader use in other sectors.

In its examination of the issue of expedited dispute resolution, UNCITRAL discussed proposals.[215] It was suggested that a solution could consist of two components: expedited arbitration procedure and adjudication.[216] At its fifty-fourth session, the UNCITRAL Commission adopted the Expedited Arbitration Rules, effective September 2021,[217] which offer model rules and contractual clauses to facilitate the use of expedited arbitration procedures that aim to reduce the cost and time of arbitration. At that same session, UNCITRAL reported that the development of model legislative provisions or contractual clauses to facilitate the widespread use of adjudication would complement this expedient initiative.[218] Accordingly, the desirability and feasibility of work on adjudication was further discussed in a colloquium requested by the Commission at the seventy-fifth session of Working Group II.[219]

7. CONCLUSIONS

The transition to clean energy is the pathway to a healthier planet and a more robust economy, but especially energy security. To achieve these goals and allow for a smooth shift in energy sources, competent legal structures must be in place. The existing institutional frameworks and trusted industry standards have fostered an attractive environment for cross-border transactions and developments. Now, as the preferred method of alternative dispute resolution, international arbitration instills confidence in parties to engage in cross-border transactions despite any cultural, geographical, and jurisdictional differences existing between nations. Accordingly, multinational projects with multi-party contracts have become an energy industry norm, for example, involving thousands of people in construction projects like offshore wind farms.[220] However, the development of a project like

---

[214] *Id.*
[215] *Id.*
[216] *Id.*
[217] United Nations General Assembly, *Report of the United Nations Commission on International Trade Law*, ¶ 189, U.N. Doc. A/76/17, August 6, 2021, UNCITRAL.
[218] *Id.*
[219] Working Group II is one of UNCITRAL's six Working Groups tasked to address issues in Dispute Settlement.
[220] *Everything You'd Like to Know About Offshore Wind Farm Construction*, IBERDROLA, https://www.iberdrola.com/about-us/our-activity/offshore-wind-energy/offshore-wind-park-construction (last visited July 28, 2023).

an offshore wind farm is complex, time-consuming, and requires millions of dollars in planning and development costs.[221] The high capital stakes, multi-party involvement, and intricacies in technical engineering make these sorts of projects highly prone to disputes.

Considering the reluctance of parties to engage in international contracts where national courts have jurisdiction, international arbitration has proven to be suitable as an alternative dispute resolution mechanism to traditional litigation. While other mechanisms, such as negotiation and mediation, employ more amicable experiences to resolve issues, parties to more complex and multifaceted agreements usually require some form of third-party participation to achieve resolution. Thus, dispute boards appear to be valuable in large-scale contracts, especially those involving long-term, anticipatory projects where parties expect to see disputes. While dispute boards do not offer finality nor guarantee a decision that both parties will deem acceptable, they assist in reducing the number of disputes that would otherwise likely proceed to arbitration.

Progressive developments in alternative dispute resolution created space for more informal and interim dispute resolution mechanisms, and the international construction industry is just one noteworthy example where dispute boards are a possible solution. Since the construction industry is highly susceptible to disputes, often arising from demands for payments or a necessary change of plans, it is crucial parties have provisions set out early on. Such provisions empower a neutral decision-maker to issue binding determinations and allow the contract's purpose and performance to continue without undue delay. Institutional organizations have paved the way in rule development to facilitate widespread acceptance and implementation of alternative dispute resolution and, recently, dispute boards.

The ICC, for example, promotes policies and develops rules that shape how business transactions should be conducted in the sphere of international business.[222] It conformed to the evolving legal landscape in international transactions and thus established a comprehensive set of provisions called the ICC Dispute Board Rules, mentioned above.[223] In addition to the ICC's contributions, the standard form contracts provided by the FIDIC are utilized in various

---

[221] *Expanding Offshore Wind to Emerging Markets*, WORLD BANK (Oct. 31, 2019), https://www.worldbank.org/en/topic/energy/publication/expanding-offshore-wind-in-emerging-markets.
[222] CORPORATE FINANCE INSTITUTE, *supra* note 85.
[223] *See Dispute Boards*, INTERNATIONAL CHAMBER OF COMMERCE (Apr. 3, 2023), https://iccwbo.org/dispute-resolution/dispute-resolution-services/adr/dispute-boards/.

jurisdictions and for several types of projects.[224] FIDIC contracts are recognized as the industry standard. Recognizing the need to address recurring project-specific issues, in 1999, FIDIC revised its contracts to include dispute adjudication boards as a principal means to resolve disputes.[225] As of 2017, a dispute board decision is a condition precedent to arbitration.[226] This means that the only matters permitted to be submitted to arbitrations are disputes that had been formally referred to the DAAB for a decision and were not subject to a final and binding decision. The effect of these revisions to the Red Book protects party relations since the avoidance function prevents one party from being a winner and one party from being a loser.

While an internationally accepted framework for dispute boards is still in its development phase, the UN expressed the long-term goal of establishing a common legislative standard similar to that of the New York Convention for recognition and enforcement of adjudicatory decisions.[227] Arbitral awards provide parties with a final and binding decision, but lengthy timelines and increasing costs associated with obtaining those awards have raised recent concerns among institutional discussions. In response to these concerns, the UN sought to address the demand for an expedited procedural framework for arbitration, and adjudication has been recognized as a useful tool in the construction industry as an interim measure.[228] The UN Working Group II examined the issue of expedited dispute resolution and proposed that the Expedited Arbitration Rules could be well complemented by adjudication since they both serve to reduce the costs and time spent by parties in receiving a determination.[229]

Currently, the principal shortcoming of dispute boards is their lack of enforceability; a beneficiary of a dispute adjudication board's decision must wait and hope for parties' voluntary compliance. Only time will tell whether an international framework (similar to that of the New York Convention) can develop. Switzerland proposed a mechanism that functions to turn an adjudicated decision into an enforceable binding award under the Convention unless challenged, which would then direct the dispute to ordinary arbitration.[230] Such a proposal offers a reasoned solution to the pressing issue in international

---

[224] *Why Use FIDIC Contracts?*, FIDIC, https://fidic.org/node/7089 (last visited July 14, 2023).
[225] *See* Bates & Torres-Fowler, *supra* note 27, at 237–64.
[226] RED BOOK § 21.1.
[227] *See supra* notes 97–103 and accompanying text.
[228] *Supra* notes 78–80 and accompanying text.
[229] *See supra* notes 210–19 and accompanying text.
[230] UNCITRAL, 54th Sess., *Swiss Proposal for Adjudication Procedure*, at 1 (June 28, 2021).

arbitration: a quick decision that still protects the integrity of thorough examination.

On the Court and International Arbitration at the Astana International Financial Center for Foreign Investors in the Oil and Gas Industry

Shalala Valiyeva[*]

ABSTRACT

Kazakhstan, the largest economy in Central Asia, has implemented measures to attract international investors and foster innovation. One of these initiatives was the establishment of the Astana International Financial Center ("AIFC") Court and the International Arbitration Center ("IAC"), as a part of Astana International Financial Centre in 2018. This study examines the innovations introduced by the AIFC, which have led to new dispute resolution mechanisms through the AIFC Court Judgments and Orders and the IAC Arbitration and Mediation Rules. The AIFC's practices can be applied to contracts in the oil and natural gas sector in Kazakhstan by including provisions establishing jurisdiction for the AIFC Court and the IAC. My analysis will thoroughly examine published Judgments and Orders and provide a comparative study of past oil and gas disputes in Kazakhstan as well as a formulation of recommendations that can benefit stakeholders in this vital sector.

Keywords: investment arbitration, international financial center, court, oil and gas industry, Kazakhstan

---

*Shalala Valiyeva is a Doctor of Juridical Science (SJD) Candidate at American University Washington College of Law; valiyeva@american.edu

1.	*INTRODUCTION*	*38*
2.	*BACKGROUND*	*39*
3.	*DIFFERENCE BETWEEN NATIONAL LEGISLATION AND AIFC REGULATIONS ON INVESTMENT DISPUTES*	*41*
4.	*ASTANA INTERNATIONAL FINANCIAL CENTER FRAMEWORK*	*44*
	A. International Arbitration Center ("IAC")	**49**
	B. Arbitrator Ethics	**52**
	C. AIFC Court	**53**
	D. Fees	**55**
5.	*The AIFC's Role in Enforceability of Arbitral Awards*	*56*
6.	*CONCLUSION*	*62*

1. **INTRODUCTION**

Since regaining its independence, the Republic of Kazakhstan has made remarkable strides in establishing a market-oriented economy that has effectively attracted foreign investors in the oil and natural gas sector. Kazakhstan holds sway in the global oil landscape, possessing nearly 3% of the world's total oil reserves.[1] The nation boasts over 170 oil fields within its territory, with oil and gas areas encompassing 62% of its landmass.[2] In January 2023, the total foreign direct investment ("FDI") stock in Kazakhstan amounted to $169.2 billion U.S. dollars, with the lion's share of these investments closely aligned with the oil and gas sector.[3] This confluence of factors casts Kazakhstan into a unique geopolitical position, with key investors from China,[4] Russia, and Western countries, particularly the United States.[5] This distinctiveness sets Kazakhstan apart from the other countries.[6]

The relationship between Kazakhstan as a rich host country with natural resources and foreign investors is different and remains complicated. Consequently, contemporary foreign investors within the oil and gas industry are

---

[1] Kazakhstan is the second largest country in Eurasia and the twelfth in the world that had proved crude oil reserves. *Energy Resource Guide, Kazakhstan – Oil & Gas*, INT'L TRADE ADMIN, https://www.trade.gov/energy-resource-guide-oil-and-gas-kazakhstan (last visited Apr. 19, 2024).
The world largest oil reserves include countries such as Venezuela (18.2%), Saudi Arabia (16%), Canada (10.4%), and others. *Oil Reserves by Country*, WISEVOTER, https://wisevoter.com/country-rankings/oil-reserves-by-country/ (last visited Apr. 19, 2024).
[2] *See* Christopher Campbell-Holt, *A Modern Business Climate in Kazakhstan for the Oil & Gas Sector: Dispute Resolution at the AIFC*, ARBITRATION JOURNAL (Feb. 3, 2021), https://journal.arbitration.ru/ru/analytics/a-modern-business-climate-in-kazakhstan-for-the-oil-gas-sector-dispute-resolution-at-the-aifc/.
[3] Every year the U.S. Department of State publishes the year report on Investment Climate Statements. *See 2023 Investment Climate Statements: Kazakhstan*, U.S. DEP'T STATE, https://www.state.gov/reports/2023-investment-climate-statements/kazakhstan/ (last visited Mar. 25, 2024).
[4] Kazakhstan became an essential destination in the oil and gas industry for Chinese investor companies because it does not require transport through the third country, there are available resources. Nearly all investors from China in Kazakhstan are state-owned enterprises ("SOE") because they dominate the natural resource sector in China.
[5] *See 2023 Investment Climate Statements: Kazakhstan*, U.S. DEP'T STATE, https://www.state.gov/reports/2023-investment-climate-statements/kazakhstan/ (last accessed Mar. 25, 2024).
[6] *See* Serik Orazgaliyev, *State intervention in Kazakhstan's energy sector: Nationalisation or participation?*, 9(2) J. EURASIAN STUDIES 143–51 (2018).

interested in the establishment of effective mechanisms for dispute resolution among involved parties. In this context, the new establishment by the Republic of Kazakhstan of the Astana International Financial Center ("AIFC") Court and the International Arbitration Centre ("IAC") has sparked heightened enthusiasm among foreign businesses and investors.

2. BACKGROUND

The establishment of the AIFC centered around the former Kazakh President Nazarbayev's '2050 Strategy' for strengthening the national legal system.[7] This strategy aimed at positioning Kazakhstan as one of the top 30 most developed countries by the year 2050.[8] Therefore, the bodies of the AIFC, the Court, and IAC have introduced a new system of justice alongside the traditional system. Currently, more than 5,700 business contracts in the industry include a clause containing the AIFC and IAC model for dispute resolution between the parties.[9] For example, in the oil and gas industry, contracts between Chevron Tengizchevroil LLP and the North Caspian Operating Company ("NCOC"), whose total contract value exceeds US $2 billion, have incorporated an AIFC clause.[10]

Kazakhstan is a signatory to Bilateral Investment Treaties ("BITs") with 43 countries,[11] a signatory to the Energy Charter Treaty, and one multilateral investment agreement with Eurasian Economic Union ("EAEU") partners. In 1995, Kazakhstan signed the New York Convention on the Recognition and Enforcement of Foreign Arbitral Awards ("the New York Convention").[12] Furthermore, in December 2001, Kazakhstan became a member of the

---

[7] *See 2023 Investment Climate Statements: Kazakhstan*, U.S. DEP'T STATE, https://www.state.gov/reports/2023-investment-climate-statements/kazakhstan/ (last accessed Mar. 25, 2024).
[8] *See* Johannes F Linn, *Kazakhstan 2050*, 6(3) GLOBAL J. EMERGING MKT. ECONS. 283, 300 (2014).
[9] *See AIFC Court and IAC present their 2021 results and future plans*, AIFC, https://court.aifc.kz/news/aifc-court-and-iac-present-their-2021-results-and-future-plans/ (last accessed Apr. 19, 2024).
[10] *See id.*
[11] *See* UNCTAD, *International Investment Agreements: Kazakhstan, United Nations Conference on Trade and Development,* https://investmentpolicy.unctad.org/international-investment-agreements/countries/107/kazakhstan (last visited April 22, 2024).
[12] *See* 330 U.N.T.S. 3, 21 U.S.T. 2517 (June 10, 1958). 'UNTC' (*United Nations Treaty Collection*), https://treaties.un.org/pages/ViewDetails.aspx?src=TREATY&mtdsg_no=XXII-1&chapter=22&clang=_en (last visited Dec. 6 2022).

International Center for the Settlement of Investment Disputes ("ICSID")[13]. In addition to international awards under the ICSID Convention, awards issued pursuant to the United Nations Commission on International Trade Law, Stockholm Chamber of Commerce, London Court of International Arbitration, or Arbitration Commission at the Kazakhstan Chamber of Commerce and Industry's arbitration rules are enforceable in Kazakhstan.[14]

As previously noted, the principal investors in Kazakhstan's oil and gas sector predominantly hail from China, Russia, and the United States ("US").[15] However, it is noteworthy that the three BITs between Kazakhstan and China, Russia, and the US exhibit divergent characteristics, particularly in the context of dispute resolution. Specifically, the BIT with China provides the provisions that in the event of a dispute, the investor must initially endeavor to seek resolution through the judicial system of the host country.[16] In other words, Article 8, section 4 of China-Kazakhstan BIT 1992 states that if the arbitral tribunal is not constituted within four months from the date of submission of the dispute to it, either party may apply to the President of the International Court of Justice to make the necessary appointments. If the President fails to do so, a senior judge of the International Court of Justice who is not affiliated with either party will be offered the appointment instead. Should this avenue prove unavailing in achieving a resolution with the host country's government, the investor retains the prerogative to initiate proceedings before an international tribunal.[17]

In terms of procedural rights, Kazakhstan's BIT with China restricts access to arbitration if claims arise in connection with expropriation or compensation, and the Treaty does not contain a cooling-off period.[18] The United States-Kazakhstan Bilateral Investment Treaty includes key features in substantive protections and procedural rights.[19] In Kazakhstan's BIT with the Russian

---

[13] *See* ICSID, *Database of Member States*, WORLD BANK, https://icsid.worldbank.org/about/member-states/database-of-member-states (last visited April 22, 2024).

[14] *See* Emmanuel Gaillard & Ilija Mitrev Penushliski, *State Compliance with Investment Awards*, 35 ICSID REV. FOREIGN INVT. L. J. 540, 544 (2020).

[15] *See 2023 Investment Climate Statements: Kazakhstan*, U.S. DEP'T STATE, https://www.state.gov/reports/2023-investment-climate-statements/kazakhstan/ (last accessed Mar. 25, 2024).

[16] *See* CHINA - KAZAKHSTAN BIT (1992), Art. 8, available in English at EDIT – Electronic Database of Investment Treaties https://edit.wti.org/document/show/2331ea73-24ec-400b-ae99-b14961526db6.

[17] *See id.* at Art. 8.4

[18] *See id.* at Art. 9.

[19] *See* KAZAKHSTAN - UNITED STATES OF AMERICA BIT (1992), available at *UNCTAD Investment Policy Hub,* UNCTAD,

Federation, an umbrella clause is excluded.[20] Moreover, in defining "investment" the BIT extends its scope to investments made prior to the BIT's entry into force.[21]

In essence, Kazakhstan's commitment to creating a favorable investment climate, coupled with its individual approach to dispute resolution in bilateral agreements, reflects a complex and adaptable structure. This not only serves the interests of the country and its investors but also strengthens the confidence of the international business community in Kazakhstan as a stable and reliable investment destination.

3. DIFFERENCE BETWEEN NATIONAL LEGISLATION AND AIFC REGULATIONS ON INVESTMENT DISPUTES

Several laws regulate foreign direct investment in Kazakhstan. This list includes the law on the entrepreneur, laws related to civil procedure, customs, government procurement, and arbitration, as well as the Customs Code of the Eurasian Economic Union, the Law on Government Procurement, and the

---

https://investmentpolicy.unctad.org/international-investment-agreements/treaties/bilateral-investment-treaties/2218/kazakhstan---united-states-of-america-bit-1992-. Substantive Protection within investment treaties suggest that they offer globally enforceable protection for the economic rights and interests of investors. This interpretation prioritizes the economic concerns of international investors and multinational enterprises over the conflicting interests, both economic and non-economic, of other entities and individuals. *See* JONATHAN BONNITCHA, SUBSTANTIVE PROTECTION UNDER INVESTMENT TREATIES A LEGAL AND ECONOMIC ANALYSIS (2014). Procedural rights mean the procedural aspect of ensuring fairness in government decision-making process, especially when such decisions have a significant impact on individuals or specific groups. Gus Van Harten, *Investment Treaty Arbitration, Procedural Fairness, and the Rule of La*, in INTERNATIONAL INVESTMENT LAW AND COMPARATIVE PUBLIC LAW (Stephan W. Schill ed., 2010).

[20] *See* KAZAKHSTAN - RUSSIAN FEDERATION BIT (1998), available at *UNCTAD Investment Policy Hub*, UNCTAD, https://investmentpolicy.unctad.org/international-investment-agreements/treaties/bilateral-investment-treaties/2209/kazakhstan---russian-federation-bit-1998-.
"An umbrella clause protects investments by bringing obligations or commitments that the host state entered into in connection with a foreign investment under the protective 'umbrella' of the BIT." Thomas Reuters, Practical Law, *Glossary Umbrella Clause* https://content.next.westlaw.com/Glossary/PracticalLaw/I43e21e821c9a11e385 78f7ccc38dcbee?transitionType=Default&contextData=(sc.Default).

[21] *See id.* at Art. 13. ("The provisions of this Agreement shall apply in respect of disputes referred to in Articles 10 and 11 of this Agreement, upon its entry into force.").

Constitutional Law on the Astana International Center.[22]

The Entrepreneurial Code delineates the basic principles governing the business environment and the interplay between the government entities and entrepreneurs. Particularly, the Entrepreneurial Code regulates both domestic and foreign business and investment activities, systematizing the rights of business entities and governing the interaction between the state and business enterprises.[23] The law further prescribes the conditions that warrant unscheduled inspections and provides a comprehensive framework for the resolution of disputes, delineating the roles and oversight responsibilities of the Business Ombudsman.[24]

Article 296.1 of this legal framework furnishes the definition of an investment dispute as "a dispute arising from contractual obligations between investors, including large investors, and government authorities in connection with the investor's investment activities."[25] Under the purview of this legislation, investment disputes can be resolved through negotiation, litigation, or international arbitration, contingent upon the pre-established dispute resolution mechanism.[26]

Diverging from this, disputes unrelated to investments are subject to the provisions of Kazakhstan's legal statutes, as articulated in Article 296.4.[27]

In March 2021, amendments to the Entrepreneurial Code brought changes to the judicial system governing investment disputes between government entities and investors in Kazakhstan.[28] These amendments established two distinct courts for this purpose, namely, the Specialized Economic Court and the Specialized Administrative Court of Nur-Sultan City.[29] The law designates the Nur-Sultan City Court to adjudicate investment disputes between government entities and

---

[22] *See* IMPROVING THE LEGAL ENVIRONMENT FOR BUSINESS AND INVESTMENT IN CENTRAL ASIA, GLOBAL RELATIONS EURASIA COMPETITIVENESS PROGRAMME, OECD 43–46 (2021), https://www.oecd.org/eurasia/Improving-LEB-CA-ENG%2020%20April.pdf.

[23] *See id.* at 39.

[24] *See id.*

[25] *See Entrepreneur Code of the Republic of Kazakhstan*, The Code of the Republic of Kazakhstan, No. 375-V ZRK, Art. 296.1, (Oct. 29, 2015), https://adilet.zan.kz/eng/docs/K1500000375 (last visited May 5, 2022).

[26] *See id.*

[27] *See id.*

[28] *Investment Climate Statements, Custom Report Excerpts: Kazakhstan, Kyrgyzstan, Tajikistan, Turkmenistan, Uzbekistan*, U.S. DEP'T OF STATE, BUREAU OF ECON. & BUS. AFFS., https://www.state.gov/report/custom/d721d10353 (last visited May 6, 2022).

[29] *See id.*

smaller investors.[30] Conversely, disputes involving larger investors and the Government of Kazakhstan fall under the exclusive jurisdiction of the Supreme Court of Kazakhstan.[31]

Article 274.4 of the Entrepreneurial Code defines "a big investor [as] an individual or legal entity making investments in the Republic of Kazakhstan in the amount of not less than two million of monthly calculation index."[32] In other words, the legislation affords big investors the direct prerogative to petition the Supreme Court, circumventing the initial court procedures. Nevertheless, the AIFC proffers distinct advantages to the parties, expediting the process by virtue of its specialized court and arbitration facilities dedicated to investment disputes. In addition, the burgeoning caseload within Kazakh state courts, stemming from diverse litigation matters, poses a potential detriment to the quality of judicial acts in investment disputes.[33]

The legal framework within the AIFC comprises statutes meticulously formulated by the host country's legislative and regulatory entities alongside those promulgated by the AIFC itself.[34]

There are two important advantages of the AIFC. First, there exists no prerequisite for a Kazakh company to undergo registration or accreditation with the AIFC when invoking the AIFC Court's jurisdiction.[35] In essence, a mutual agreement between local and/or foreign persons or companies suffices for the resolution of disputes within the AIFC Court. Second, the parties may opt for the application of Kazakh legislation, thereby obviating the need for recourse to English law or AIFC law for dispute resolution.[36]

---

[30] *See id.*
[31] *See Investment Disputes*, KAZAKH INV. NAT'L CO., https://invest.gov.kz/invest-guide/support/investment-activity/investment-disputes (last visited May 5, 2022).
[32] *See Entrepreneur Code of the Republic of Kazakhstan*, The Code of the Republic of Kazakhstan, No. 375-V ZRK, Art. 274.4, (Oct. 29, 2015), https://adilet.zan.kz/eng/docs/K1500000375 (last visited May 5, 2022).
[33] *See id.*
[34] *See* Nicolás Zambrana-Tévar, *The Court of the Astana International Financial Center in the Wake of Its Predecessors,* 1 ERASMUS L. REV. 122, 135 (2019).
[35] *See id.* at 127.
[36] *Contra* Ardak Idayatova & Farukh Iminov, *Litigation and Enforcement in Kazakhstan: Overview,* AEQUITAS (Sept. 1, 2022), https://uk.practicallaw.thomsonreuters.com/w-019-2504?transitionType=Default&contextData=(sc.Default)&firstPage=true (stating that this creates disadvantages for the parties because the AIFC judges are foreign nationals and do not have knowledge about Kazakhstan legislation, they will interpret the legislation based on the opinions of lawyers qualified under the legislation of the Republic of Kazakhstan).

4. ASTANA INTERNATIONAL FINANCIAL CENTER FRAMEWORK

To protect investors' rights within its jurisdiction, the Republic of Kazakhstan established an independent judicial entity named the AIFC with a distinct legal framework based on English law principles. The AIFC is the first institution in Central Asia to do so.[37] English law is a preferred choice due to its extensive experience in handling international dispute resolutions.[38]

The AIFC has officially operated since 2018 in the city of Astana.[39] This initiative was patterned after the Dubai International Financial Center, with the overarching objective of positioning the Center as a pivotal financial hub in Central Asia.[40] The primary aim is to foster economic diversification in Kazakhstan and provide a platform to enter the list of the top 30 developed countries by the year 2050.[41] Within the legal framework of the AIFC, two vital entities have been instituted: The AIFC Court and the IAC.

The AIFC Court and IAC have achieved international recognition by adjudicating cases from a variety of regions, including the Commonwealth of Independent State ("CIS") countries, China, India, and 15 Belt and Road Initiative countries.[42] The AIFC law and the laws of Kazakhstan meticulously regulate the procedural guidelines for dispute resolution. Notably, the AIFC ensures an enforcement mechanism whereby the judgments of the Court and arbitration awards are enforced on Kazakhstan's territory.[43] To satisfy the parties involved,

---

[37] *Annual Report on The Activities of the Astana International Financial Center 2021*, AIFC (2021), https://aifc.kz/uploads/Annual%20Report/AIFC%20AR%202021%20ENG.pdf.
[38] *See id.* at 17.
[39] *See id.*
[40] *See id.*
[41] *See* Phillip Kim, Herbert Smith Freehills, *Why arbitrate at the Astana International Financial Centre?,* KLUWER ARBITRATION BLOG (Sept. 19, 2018), http://arbitrationblog.kluwerarbitration.com/2018/09/19/why-arbitrate-at-the-astana-international-financial-centre (last visited Dec. 5, 2022).
[42] *See Countries of the Belt and Road Initiative (BRI),* GREEN FIN. & DEV. CTR., https://greenfdc.org/countries-of-the-belt-and-road-initiative-bri (last visited Dec. 6, 2022). Note: 146 countries joined the Belt and Road Initiative ("BRI") in March 2022 by signing the Memorandum of Understanding with China. 43 countries are in Sub-Saharan Africa, 34 BRI countries are in Europe & Central Asia (including 18 countries of the European Union (EU) that are part of the BRI), 25 BRI countries are in East Asia & Pacific, 20 BRI countries are in Latin America & Caribbean, 18 BRI countries in Middle East & North Africa, 6 countries are in Southeast Asia.
[43] *Annual Report on The Activities of the Astana International Financial Center 2021*, AIFC 32 (2021), https://aifc.kz/uploads/Annual%20Report/AIFC%20AR%202021%20ENG.pdf.

the AIFC Court undertakes distinctive measures to guarantee adherence to the prescribed judgment, interacting directly with enforcement authorities, thus circumventing the need for recourse to the national courts.

In stark contrast to the local court system, the AIFC Court and the IAC are independent self-managed institutions that are beyond the purview of any court within Kazakhstan, so the final decisions of these bodies are immune from reversal by any Kazakhstan court.[44] Furthermore, the AIFC Court and the IAC maintain an ongoing collaboration with the Supreme Court of Kazakhstan, engaging in activities such as meetings, lectures, and training sessions as part of their cooperative efforts.[45]

The AIFC Court issues judgments pertaining to the enforcement and recognition of arbitral awards by the IAC.[46] In cases where a party abstains from voluntary enforcement of the arbitral award, the AIFC Court offers a simplified procedure for enforcing said arbitral award.[47] A notable distinction between the AIFC Court and the IAC is confidentiality. While the judgments rendered by the AIFC Court are made publicly accessible on the official AIFC website, disputes adjudicated by the IAC are not public.[48]

By June 7, 2023, the AIFC Court and the IAC successfully completed and enforced 2,174 cases.[49] Among these cases, 64 represent AIFC Court judgements (constituting 3%), 415 pertain to arbitration awards (making up 19%), and 1695 are associated with mediation settlements (comprising 78%).[50] In 2023 alone, there has been a noteworthy growth in case volume, with 533 cases resolved.[51] This figure represents that 24.5% of all cases brought before the AIFC Court and the IAC, since operations began on January 1, 2018, were resolved and enforced in 2023 alone, reflecting the continued effectiveness and impact of the AIFC Court and the IAC in handling legal matters.[52]

---

[44] *Id.*
[45] *Welcome to AIFC*, AIFC, https://aifc.kz (last visited Dec. 6, 2022).
[46] *AIFC Court Enforcement*, AIFC, https://court.aifc.kz/en/enforcement (last visited May 5, 2022).
[47] *See Id.*
[48] *See Judgments,* AIFC, https://court.aifc.kz/en/judgments; *Welcome to the International Arbitration Centre,* IAC, AIFC, https://iac.aifc.kz/en.
[49] *See More than 2,100 cases resolved and enforced by the AIFC Court and IAC,* AIFC COURT (June 7, 2023), https:// court.aifc.kz/en/news/more-than-2-100-cases-resolved-and-enforced-by-the-aifc-court-and-iac (last visited Nov. 12, 2023).
[50] *See id.*
[51] *See id.*
[52] *See id.*

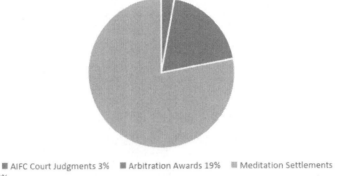

■ AIFC Court Judgments 3%   ■ Arbitration Awards 19%   ■ Meditation Settlements 78%

Figure 1: AIFC Court and IAC cases completed and enforced by 7 June 2023. Number of cases is 2,174.[53]

The AIFC Court and the IAC discussed and covered various business issues, most of which related to contracts (43.8%).[54] Other common issues included construction (15.8%), employment (15%), company (10.5%), transport (6%), property (4%), logistics (3%), and public private partnership ("PPP") (2%) matters.[55]

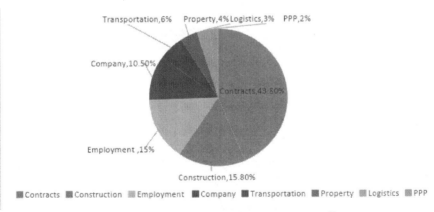

■ Contracts ■ Construction ■ Employment ■ Company ■ Transportation ■ Property ■ Logistics ■ PPP

Figure 2. Type of cases that AIFC Court and IAC considered.[56]

In 97.7% of cases, the parties involved conducted business in Kazakhstan and

---

[53] *See id.*
[54] *See id.* (43.8% of matters involved contracts, often related to non-payments and failure to fulfill contractual obligations).
[55] *See id.*
[56] *See id.*

voluntarily chose to arbitrate in the AIFC Court and the IAC.[57] The AIFC and the IAC applied Kazakh law in 97.5% of these cases and AIFC law in 2.3% of cases.[58]

The table below provides a concise overview of key statistics related to the AIFC Court and the IAC, covering claim values, investor distribution, geographic representation, gender diversity among arbitrators and staff, and global representation of lawyers registered with the AIFC Court.[59]

Highest Claim Value	USD 330 million[60]
Distribution of Claim Values	Majority in multi-millions of US Dollars ("USD")
Percentage of Cases Involving Foreign Investors	48%
Countries Represented	23 (including Eurasian countries, China, UAE, India)
Arbitrators' Gender Distribution	75% women (IAC)
Staff Gender Distribution	80% women (AIFC Court and IAC)
AIFC Court Registrants	500 lawyers from 30 countries (32 jurisdictions) on 6 continents

Table 1. Key statistics for 2023.[61]

At the Astana Finance Day 2023 events held on June 7, 2023, the AIFC Court and IAC introduced three novel initiatives.[62] These endeavors aimed to strengthen engagement with their user base and bolster their role in advancing Kazakhstan's appeal as a hub for commercial dispute resolution and investment.[63]

The first initiative is "The AIFC Court and IAC Eurasia Expansion Initiative," which involves the physical presence of the AIFC Court and the IAC

---

[57] *See id.*
[58] *See id.*
[59] *See id.*
[60] *See BCLP Acts in the Largest Case in History of Astana International Financial Centre Court*, BRYAN CAVE LEIGHTON PAISNER LLP (June 1, 2023), https://www.bclplaw.com/en-US/events-insights-news/bclp-acts-in-the-largest-case-in-history-of-astana-international-financial-centre-court.html.
[61] *See More than 2,100 Cases Resolved and Enforced by the AIFC Court and IAC*, *supra* note 49.
[62] *See id.*; *see also GRATA International Will Participate in the Astana Finance Days*, GRATA INTERNATIONAL (June 2, 2023), https://gratanet.com/news/grata-international-will-participate-in-the-astana-finance-days.
[63] *See More than 2,100 Cases Resolved and Enforced by the AIFC Court and IAC*, *supra* note 49.

abroad. New AIFC Court and IAC have established premises in eight countries across Eurasia: Armenia, Azerbaijan, Georgia, Kyrgyzstan, Tajikistan, Turkmenistan, and Uzbekistan.[64] The purpose of this initiative is to provide access to the AIFC Court and the IAC and help businesses with ties to Kazakhstan resolve commercial disputes more conveniently.[65]

The second initiative is titled the "IAC Chambers."[66] IAC Chambers works with a global group called International Arbitration Centre Alliance, which includes arbitration centers worldwide.[67] IAC Chambers functions as a "one-stop shop" for resolving disputes at the AIFC Court and the IAC.[68] IAC Chambers has great facilities and digital tools for hearings, and can handle complex cases with multiple parties and locations— proceedings may be held in person, hybrid, and virtual from anywhere in the world.[69]

The third initiative is the "AIFC Court and IAC Training Center."[70] The AIFC Court and the IAC Training Center in Kazakhstan offer first-class training under the guidance of experts from the United Kingdom ("UK"), the US, and Germany, with trainers from renowned universities including Cambridge and University College London.[71] The courses, conducted in English, focus on dispute resolution for lawyers, arbitrators, mediators, and judges.[72] More than 100 Kazakh law students have completed the international internship program.[73] Every year, the IAC holds a preliminary competition for Central Asia in Vienna, and the AIFC Court holds a commercial training competition in October.[74] To date, more than 3,000 Kazakhstani law students, lawyers, civil servants, judges, and business representatives have been trained at these institutions.[75]

In summary, the creation of the AIFC in Kazakhstan shows a strong dedication to protecting investors and encouraging economic variety. The AIFC's effective management of complex legal issues and its creative ideas make it a significant player in the worldwide financial scene.

---

[64] *See id.*
[65] *See id.*
[66] *See id.*
[67] *See id.*
[68] *Id.*
[69] *See id.*
[70] *Id.*
[71] *See id.*
[72] *See id.*
[73] *See id.*
[74] *See id.*
[75] *See id.*

A. International Arbitration Center ("IAC")

The establishment of the IAC has succeeded in attracting investors to the oil and gas sector. This allure is attributable to the fact that the AIFC Court offers important facilities that meet the standards of foreign investors.

The IAC employs international best practices for dispute resolution, utilizing a panel of esteemed international arbitrators and mediators with expertise in various domains "in commercial law, including oil and gas, trade, construction, energy, financial services, banking, Islamic finance, insurance, and intellectual property."[76] According to data as of March, 2024, the IAC houses 44 international arbitrators and mediators, who have collectively handled 2,349 arbitration and mediation cases and 27 commercial disputes between parties from 27 countries.[77] The awards issued through IAC arbitration proceedings hold recognition and enforceability not only within Kazakhstan but also at the international level.[78]

Historically, the Stockholm Chamber of Commerce (the "SCC") and the ICSID heard most disputes between foreign investors and Kazakhstan that related to the oil and gas industry.[79] In Kazakhstan, arbitral awards from various institutions, including the London Court of International Arbitration ("LCIA"), the Arbitration Institute of the SCC, the Grain and Feed Trade Association, and the ICC, are commonly enforced.[80] The primary legal framework for this enforcement is the New York Convention, which Kazakhstan has ratified.[81]

---

[76] *See AIFC Court and IAC Present Their 2021 Results and Future Plans*, AIFC (Dec. 29, 2021, 1:29 PM), https://court.aifc.kz/en/news/aifc-court-and-iac-present-their-2021-results-and-future-plans.

[77] *See Welcome to the International Arbitration Center*, IAC, https://iac.aifc.kz/en (last visited Mar. 2, 2024).

[78] *See AIFC Court and IAC Present Their 2021 Results and Future Plans*, *supra* note 76.

[79] *See, e.g.,* Biedermann Int'l, Inc. v. Kazakhstan, (SCC Arbitration V (97/1996)), Award, Aug. 2, 1999; CCL v. Kazakhstan, (SCC Arbitration V (122/2001)), Award, Jan. 1, 2004; Anatolie Stati and Others v. Kazakhstan (SCC Arbitration V (116/2010)), Award, Dec. 19, 2013; *Cases*, ICSID, https://icsid.worldbank.org/cases/case-database (last visited Apr. 19, 2024) (use "Filter by" function and select Kazakhstan under "Respondent(s) Nationality(ies)").

[80] *See* Saniya Perzadayeva, *Top 5 'Must-Knows' To Enforce Arbitral Award in Kazakhstan*, CONVENTUS LAW (June 3, 2020), https://conventuslaw.com/report/top-5-must-knows-to-enforce-arbitral-award-in/.

[81] *See Id.* Note: Locally, the enforcement process is governed by key legislative acts: Civil Procedural Code of Kazakhstan (October 13, 2015), Law 'On Arbitration' (April 8, 2016), Law 'On Enforcement Proceedings and Status of Court Enforcement Officers' (April 2, 2010). The enforcement of arbitral awards

In comparison, a key aspect of the AIFC Rules that enhances their appeal is their suitability for commercial parties looking for quick dispute resolution, especially those with interests in Kazakhstan. These Rules closely resemble the content and structure of rules followed by top arbitration institutions like the Hong Kong International Arbitration Center ("HKIAC")[82] and the LCIA.[83] Both sets of rules cover similar procedures, such as initiating arbitration proceedings, appointing arbitrators, applying for provisional or emergency relief, combining proceedings, and adding parties to the arbitration.[84]

Even though it might require some additional interpretive support, the Arbitration and Mediation Rules at the IAC contain provisions to regulate the arbitration process effectively.[85]

In assessing the AIFC International Arbitration Center Arbitration and Mediation Rules of 2022, it is essential to compare these provisions and clauses with those found in various other international arbitration rules.[86] The following discussion evaluates the AIFC International Arbitration Center Arbitration and Mediation Rules of 2022 by comparing them to reveal both similarities and differences, which could affect the interpretation and application of the AIFC rules, especially in managing disputes involving multiple treaties.

In Article 2 of the Rules on Arbitration and Mediation at the IAC, the term "overriding objective" refers to the core principle of ensuring a tribunal's

---

in Kazakhstan involves two main steps:
  A. Recognition and Enforcement Order: The first step is to seek recognition and enforcement of the arbitral award within a competent local court. This involves obtaining an enforcement order from the court.
  B. Actual Enforcement: Following the issuance of the enforcement order, the second step is the actual enforcement of the arbitral award. This is carried out by a court officer, who ensures that the terms of the award are implemented.

[82] *See* H.K. Int'l Arb. Ctr. [HKIAC], *Administered Arbitration Rules* (Nov. 1, 2018).

[83] *See* London Ct. of Int'l Arb. [LCIA], *Arbitration Rules* (Dec. 1, 2023).

[84] *See* H.K. Int'l Arb. Ctr. [HKIAC], *Administered Arbitration Rules* (Nov. 1, 2018); London Court of International Arbitration [LCIA], *Arbitration Rules* (Dec. 1, 2023).

[85] *See* Astana Int'l Fin. Ctr. [AIFC] Int'l Arb. Ctr., *Rules on Arbitration and Mediation at the International Arbitration Centre, Astana* (Sept. 19, 2022), https://aifc.kz/files/legals/75/file/iac-rules-no-cover.pdf (last accessed: Nov. 13, 2023).

[86] *See* Philip Kim & Herbert Smith Freehills, *Why arbitrate at the Astana International Financial Centre?*, KLUWER ARBITRATION BLOG (Sept. 19, 2018), http://arbitrationblog.kluwerarbitration.com/2018/09/19/why-arbitrate-at-the-astana-international-financial-centre/.

impartial and expeditious resolution of disputes while minimizing unwarranted delays and excessive costs.[87] This provision bears similarities to Section 33 of the English Arbitration Act of 1996.[88] Nevertheless, a noteworthy distinction arises in that the Act imposes a general duty on the Tribunal concerning various aspects, including the conduct of arbitral proceedings, decisions regarding procedural and evidentiary matters, and the exercise of all other conferred powers.[89]

Given that the legal frameworks for arbitration in Kazakhstan are rooted in the common law system, it is unclear how arbitrators within the IAC would interpret and apply the regulations set forth in Article 2.[90] Despite the comprehensive nature of Article 2 in comparison to Section 33, its impact on arbitration practice might not be substantial because Article 2 embodies the standard elements of the arbitration process, and the specific wording of the text does not unequivocally impose a more stringent "duty."[91]

Another noteworthy comparison lies in relation to Article 6 of the Rules, which discusses "joinder and consolidation."[92] Articles 6.8 and 6.9 of the Rules do not explicitly clarify whether arbitrations involving multiple contracts should be initiated through a "single request" or through "separate requests" with later consolidation.[93] In contrast, the Singapore International Arbitration Centre's Rule 6 offers a more expansive explanation regarding the filing of a Notice of Arbitration covering multiple agreements.[94] This divergent approach is significant, particularly considering the increasing complexity of commercial disputes and alignment with international organizations.[95]

This difference is important to all parties to the arbitration as they must remain cognizant of the specific conditions governing the submission of a Notice

---

[87] *See* Astana Int'l Fin. Ctr. [AIFC] Int'l Arb. Ctr., *Rules on Arbitration and Mediation at the International Arbitration Centre, Astana,* Art. 2.1 (Sept. 19, 2022).
[88] *See* Astana Int'l Fin. Ctr. [AIFC] Int'l Arb. Ctr., *Rules on Arbitration and Mediation at the International Arbitration Centre, Astana,* Art. 2.1 (Sept. 19, 2022); Arbitration Act 1996, c. 23 (UK).
[89] *See* Arbitration Act 1996, c. 23 (UK).
[90] *See* Astana Int'l Fin. Ctr. [AIFC] Int'l Arb. Ctr., *Rules on Arbitration and Mediation at the International Arbitration Centre, Astana,* Art. 2 (Sept. 19, 2022).
[91] *See id.*
[92] *See* Astana Int'l Fin. Ctr. [AIFC] Int'l Arb. Ctr., *Rules on Arbitration and Mediation at the International Arbitration Centre, Astana,* Art. 6 (Sept. 19, 2022).
[93] *See id.*
[94] *See* Sing. Int'l Arb. Ctr. [SIAC], *Arbitration Rules of the SIAC* (Aug. 1, 2016).
[95] *See* Astana Int'l Fin. Ctr. [AIFC] Int'l Arb. Ctr., *Rules on Arbitration and Mediation at the International Arbitration Centre, Astana,* Art. 6 (Sept. 19, 2022); Sing. Int'l Arb. Ctr. [SIAC], *Arbitration Rules of the SIAC* (Aug. 1, 2016).

of Arbitration under each contract, vis-à-vis the option of a single notice covering all contracts.

In sum, a comparative examination of the AIFC IAC Arbitration and Mediation Rules of 2022, particularly in relation to Article 2 and Article 6, highlights both congruities and divergences with other international arbitration rules. These disparities hold potential implications for interpreting and applying these rules within the context of the IAC and the procedural considerations for handling disputes involving multiple contracts.

B. Arbitrator Ethics

The ethical standards governing the conduct of arbitrators play a pivotal role in maintaining the integrity and fairness of the arbitration process.[96] Article 9 of the IAC rules underscores the paramount principles of independence and impartiality in the appointment of arbitrators, and it imposes obligations on arbitrators to disclose any information that may reasonably cast doubt on their independence or impartiality.[97] These principles are generally accepted as fundamental to the practice of arbitration.

However, while the IAC rules lay out these general principles, some other arbitration rules take a more expansive approach in providing guidance on how these principles should be applied. For instance, the Korean Commercial Arbitration Board adopted a Code of Ethics of Arbitrators "to ensure impartiality and independence of the arbitration tribunal" consisting of seven (7) articles.[98]

Similarly, the International Chamber of Commerce ("ICC") offers valuable insights through Section III of its "Notes to Parties and Arbitral Tribunals on the Conduct of Arbitration."[99] These notes provide comprehensive guidance on the conduct of arbitration proceedings.[100] They cover various aspects, including the duties and responsibilities of arbitrators, the role of the arbitral tribunal, and the management of the arbitral process.[101] These notes aim at ensuring that the

---

[96] *See* Astana Int'l Fin. Ctr. [AIFC] Int'l Arb. Ctr., *Rules on Arbitration and Mediation at the International Arbitration Centre, Astana,* Art. 9 (Sept. 19, 2022).
[97] *See id.*
[98] *See* Korean Commercial Arbitration Board [KCAB], *KCAB Code of Ethics for Arbitrators.*
[99] *See* International Chamber of Commerce [ICC] International Court of Arbitration, *Notes to Parties and Arbitral Tribunals on the Conduct of the Arbitration* (Dec. 29, 2020), https://iccwbo.org/news-publications/arbitration-adr-rules-and-tools/note-parties-arbitral-tribunals-conduct-arbitration/#single-hero-document.
[100] *See id.*
[101] *See id.*

arbitration process stays fair, efficient, and transparent.[102]

Ethical considerations in arbitration, particularly concerning the independence and impartiality of arbitrators, uphold the integrity of the arbitration process.

While Article 9 of the IAC rules outlines these fundamental principles, other arbitration rules, such as those followed by the Korean Commercial Arbitration and the ICC, offer more detailed and specific guidance on the application and interpretation of these principles in practice.[103] This additional guidance contributes to a clearer understanding of the ethical standards expected of arbitrators and the fair and just conduct of arbitration proceedings.[104]

C. AIFC Court

The AIFC Court operates under a set of procedural rules that combine elements of English common law procedures and international best practices. Since its establishment, the Court has appointed nine judges from jurisdictions where English is the primary language of legal proceedings.[105] This selection of judges with a background in English common law contributes to the application of a legal framework familiar to international users of the AIFC Court.[106] Currently, the AIFC has one Chief Justice along with eight other Justices.[107] Six Justices are judges and have eligibility to hear cases in the AIFC Court of First Instance and the Court of Appeal.[108] The AIFC Court also houses Justices specialized in small claims cases.[109] In terms of Judgments & Orders, a total of 555 lawyers are registered for rights of audience, hailing from 32 diverse jurisdictions, and actively engaged in resolving commercial disputes spanning 27 different countries.[110]

Article 13 of the AIFC Constitutional Statute of the Republic of Kazakhstan is of particular significance in understanding the AIFC Court's legal position.[111]

---

[102] *See id.*
[103] *See supra* notes 98–102 and accompanying text.
[104] Astana Int'l Fin. Ctr. [AIFC] Int'l Arb. Ctr., *Rules on Arbitration and Mediation at the International Arbitration Centre, Astana*, Art. 6 (Sept. 19, 2022).
[105] *See Who We Are*, AIFC (Mar. 27, 2024), https://court.aifc.kz/en/who-we-are.
[106] *See generally Constitutional Statute of the Republic of Kazakhstan on the Astana International Financial Centre*, AIFC (Dec. 30, 2022).
[107] *See Who We Are*, AIFC (Mar. 27, 2024), https://court.aifc.kz/en/who-we-are.
[108] *See id.*
[109] *See id.*
[110] *See Welcome to the AIFC Court*, AIFC (Nov. 13, 2023), https://court.aifc.kz/en.
[111] *See Constitutional Statute of the Republic of Kazakhstan on the Astana International Centre*, AIFC (Nov. 13, 2023),

Article 13 explicitly states the distinctiveness of the AIFC Court from Kazakhstan's domestic judicial system, emphasizing its autonomy.[112] Moreover, under Article 13.4, the AIFC Court lacks jurisdiction over criminal and administrative cases.[113] Instead, it confines its competence to specific categories of disputes, including:

1. Disputes between AIFC Participants, AIFC Participants and AIFC Bodies, and disputes involving an AIFC Participant or AIFC Body and its expatriate Employees.
2. Disputes pertaining to activities conducted within the AIFC and governed by the AIFC's enacted laws.
3. Disputes that have been transferred to the AIFC Court through a mutual agreement between the parties involved.[114]

The AIFC Court is organized into two distinct segments: the Court of First Instance and the Court of Appeal.[115] The Court of First Instance includes a specialized division, known as the Small Claims Court, which efficiently deals with less complex cases.[116] The Court of Appeal, on the other hand, possesses exclusive jurisdiction over disputes for which all the parties involved have a written agreement including the Court of Appeal as the final forum for their disputes.[117]

Article 24.4 of the AIFC IAC Arbitration and Mediation Rules of 2022 grants parties the option, with the approval of the Tribunal, to request the AIFC Court of First Instance to issue an order enforcing the Tribunal's decision or Award, or specific portions thereof.[118] This mechanism underscores the AIFC Court's function in supporting and facilitating the enforcement of arbitral awards or decisions, contributing to the overall effectiveness of the dispute resolution process within the AIFC jurisdiction.

---

https://aifc.kz/files/legals/7/file/constitutional-statute-on-the-aifc-with-amendments-as-of-30-december-2022.pdf.

[112] *See id.*
[113] *See id.*
[114] *See id.*
[115] *See id.*
[116] *An Introduction*, AIFC (Nov. 13, 2023), https://court.aifc.kz/en/an-introduction.
[117] *See id.*
[118] *See Rules on Arbitration and Mediation at the International Arbitration Centre, Astana 2022 (IAC Rules)*, AIFC (Nov. 12, 2023), https://aifc.kz/files/legals/75/file/iac-rules-no-cover.pdf.

D. Fees

Potential parties will also be interested in AIFC Arbitration and Court fees. Per an announcement on the AIFC Court, "[a]ll Parties to a contract which was agreed before 1 April 2023 and included the AIFC Court in the contract for dispute resolution will not have to pay the above application fees and will receive free administration of all case work at the AIFC Court under that contract."[119] The AIFC Court Regulations[120] and the IAC Rules[121] contain provisions on Court fees. However, there is little publicly available information on these Court fees. For example, the company "Grata International" shared that in their case in which there was a total amount of claims exceeding 4 million USD, it paid for an arbitrator's service cost of 20,000 USD; the company thereafter strongly recommended adding the AIFC jurisdiction clause in the company's contracts given the cost advantage provided for in the announcement by the AIFC.[122] The company provided a cost comparison with the ICC Arbitration, which would cost around 250,000 USD (attorney fees, travel expenses excluded) for claims amounting to more than 3 million USD.[123]

On April 1, 2023, the Court published "Practice Direction NO. 1: FEES."[124] The Chief Justice of the AIFC approved the fees under the Article 18(2)(e) and Article 30 of the AIFC Court Regulations of 2017.[125] The information includes relevant fees in accordance with the claim value.[126]

---

[119] COURT PRACTICE DIRECTION NO. 1: FEES, AIFC (2023), https://court.aifc.kz/uploads/AIFC%20Court%20Practice%20Direction%20No.%201%20Fees.pdf.

[120] *See* AIFC FEES RULES, AIFC RULES NO. FR0007 (2017).

[121] *See Rules on Arbitration and Mediation at the International Arbitration Centre*, Astana 2022 (IAC Rules), AIFC (Nov. 12, 2023), https://aifc.kz/files/legals/75/file/iac-rules-no-cover.pdf.

[122] *See The AIF Court and the IAC - an oasis of justice recommended for companies from the CIS countries for transnational transactions*, GRATA INTERNATIONAL (Nov. 25, 2021), https://gratanet.com/news/the-aifc-court-and-the-iac.

[123] *See id.*

[124] *See* COURT PRACTICE DIRECTION NO.1: FEES, *supra* note 119.

[125] *See id.*

[126] *See id.*

PRACTICE DIRECTION NO. 1: FEES

Claim value	AIFC Court Fees
< KZT 1.5 million / (USD 3,333)	No fee
KZT 1.5 million+ / (USD 3,334+)	Individual (0.5%) / legal entity (1.5%)
KZT 4.5 billion+ / (USD 10 million+)	KZT 23,000,000 / (USD 50,000) (Fixed fee)
	KZT 68,000,000 / (USD 150,000) (Fixed fee)
Non-monetary claim	KZT 45,000 / (USD 100) (Fixed fee)
Permission to appeal / Appeal	No fee
Execution order	No fee

Table 2. The Practice Direction by the AIFC Court describes the fees that come into effect on 1 April 2023. Source: AIFC Court Practice Direction No. 1: Fees[127]

Based on information available in publicly shared sources and demonstrated practices, the AIFC offers notable benefits in the arena of dispute resolution–particularly when dealing with substantial sums typically associated with long-term contracts in the oil and gas sector. Various facets of the AIFC's legal framework and dispute resolution mechanisms root these advantages.

5. The AIFC's Role in Enforceability of Arbitral Awards

Ease of enforcement is one of the advantages of arbitration over litigation for international disputes. Even though Kazakhstan is a party of the New York Convention, and local legislation supports the enforcement of arbitration awards, the AIFC Court has exclusive jurisdiction over the enforcement of the arbitration decisions.[128]

Under Article 24.4 Interim Relief of the Arbitration and Mediation Rules of IAC, the party awarded can get permission from the Tribunal to request the AIFC Court of First Instance to order the enforcement of provisional relief or an Award.[129] As mentioned above, the AIFC Court is an independent court composed

---

[127] *See id.*

[128] *See Starting a business in AIFC*, AIFC, https://aifc.kz/en/starting-a-business-in-aifc-2 (last visited Apr. 19, 2024); *Court Regulations, Resolution of the AIFC Management Council*, AIFC (Nov. 12, 2023), https://court.aifc.kz/files/legals/68/file/3.-legislation-aifc-court-regulations-2017.pdf.

[129] *See* Rules on Arbitration and Mediation at the International Arbitration Centre, Astana 2022 (IAC Rules), AIFC (Nov. 12, 2023).

of judges with common law experience.[130] This opportunity may prove useful for investors in oil and gas industry regarding the enforcement action of an Award on the territory of Kazakhstan for the following reasons.[131] First, the AIFC Court's decisions are enforceable in Kazakhstan and are on par with decisions of Kazakhstan's national courts.[132] Second, even though Kazakhstan has acceded to the New York Convention on the Recognition and Enforcement of Foreign Arbitral Awards in 1995, this Convention has not been ratified.[133] The Constitution of the Republic of Kazakhstan states that ratified international treaties take precedence over Kazakhstan's domestic laws, so ratification might lead to the enforceability of foreign awards based on the reciprocity principle.[134] Here, Kazakhstan law states that any international treaty that is acceded to equates

---

[130] *See* AIFC Court Regulations, Resolution of the AIFC Management Council, AIFC (Nov. 12, 2023), https://court.aifc.kz/files/legals/68/file/3.-legislation-aifc-court-regulations-2017.pdf.

[131] *See* Rules on Arbitration and Mediation, supra note 129.

[132] *See Constitutional State of the Republic of Kazakhstan on the Astana International Financial Centre*, AIFC, https://aifc.kz/files/legals/7/file/constitutional-statute-on-the-aifc-with-amendments-as-of-30-december-2022.pdf.

[133] *See Status:* UNCITRAL, *Convention on the Recognition and Enforcement of Foreign Arbitral Awards (New York, 1958) (the "New York Convention), Kazakhstan,* https://uncitral.un.org/en/texts/arbitration/conventions/foreign_arbitral_awards/status2, (last accessed May 5, 2024); *see also* Law firm "AEQUITAS". (2019, July 15). Call for Ratification of the New York and European Conventions: Silence Annoying Investors and the Law (Valikhan Shaikenov, LL.M., Georgetown University, Partner and Head of Dispute Resolution Practice at AEQUITAS Law Firm, Almaty). Information system PARAGRAPH.
(original: Юридическая фирма «AEQUITAS», 'Призыв к ратификации Нью-Йоркской и Европейской конвенций: молчание, раздражающее инвесторов и право (Валихан Шайкенов, магистр права Джорджтаунского университета, партнер и глава практики по разрешению споров юридической фирмы AEQUITAS, Алматы)' (*Информационная система ПАРАГРАФ*, 15 July 2019), https://online.zakon.kz/Document/?doc_id=37669169&pos=6;-106#pos=6;-106.
Note: Some source such as a report by the Department of State describe this as "ratified". However, according to the sources from Kazakhstan it has been signed but not ratified and discussion still is going on this point. Along with the NY Convention there are still discussions on non-ratification of the European Convention on International Commercial Arbitration (1961).

[134] Convention on the Recognition and Enforcement of Foreign Arbitral Awards, June 10, 1958, 338 U.N.T.S. 38.

with a ratified international treaty by meaning of a legislative act.[135] Since the New York Convention is acceded by a Presidential decree and not a legislative act, the Convention cannot be considered a ratified international treaty in Kazakhstan.[136]

Furthermore, there is not a separate rule specifically addressing the implementation of the New York Convention. Instead, the regulations in place include the Arbitration Law of April 8, 2016 (Chapter 7)[137] and the Civil Procedural Code of October 31, 2015 (Chapter 56),[138] which govern the recognition and enforcement of arbitration awards. The enforcement process for arbitration awards in the national courts of Kazakhstan requires a court-issued ruling to validate and enforce the award, an inherent drawback to the national court system.[139] This ruling essentially acts as a mechanism for executing the award but necessitates a judicial review to determine its applicability.

Here are some examples of Judgments and Orders issued by AIFC that provide insight into its operational procedures. In a case involving *Seha Corporation*, a Korean energy firm-initiated litigation against its business partner in Kazakhstan due to issues arising from a joint oil development project.[140] The dispute was referred to the ICC for arbitration.[141] The arbitral tribunal directed the Kazakhstani company to provide compensation amounting to approximately 17 billion South Korean Won and to cover half of the legal expenses incurred by the Korean company.[142] Legal representation for Seha Corporation, the firm Kim & Chang, stressed the significance of opting for arbitration proceedings, as they believed that Kazakhstani state courts inconsistently render equitable judgments for foreign investors involved in substantial natural resource investments.[143] In

---

[135] Constitution of the Republic of Kazakhstan (adopted Sept. 7, 1995), art. 4, ¶ 3, Refworld, https://www.refworld.org/legal/legislation/natlegbod/1995/en/1753.
[136] A. Mukhametkalikyzy, *Hidden Impediments Await Foreign Parties Seeking to Enforce Arbitral Awards in Kazakhstan*, KLUWER ARBITRATION BLOG (Apr. 21, 2020), http://arbitrationblog.kluwerarbitration.com/2020/04/01/hidden-impediments-await-foreign-parties-seeking-to-enforce-arbitral-awards-in-kazakhstan/.
[137] Arbitration Law of April 8, 2016 (Chapter 7).
[138] Civil Procedural Code of October 31, 2015 (Chapter 56, Article 464-503).
[139] Mukhametkalikyzy, *supra* note 136.
[140] Kim Da-ye, *Korean energy firm wins suit against Kazakhstan company*, THE KOREA TIMES (June 3, 2014, 4:22 PM), https://www.koreatimes.co.kr/www/nation/2024/04/113_158401.html.
[141] *Id.*
[142] *Id.*; "won" is the official currency in South Korea, currently, US $1= 1,330.34 won, https://www.forbes.com/advisor/money-transfer/currency-converter/usd-krw/?amount=1 (last visited Mar. 16, 2024).
[143] *See* Kim Da-ye, *supra* note 140.

light of these circumstances, the Supreme Court of Kazakhstan, through its ruling dated December 23, 2015, postponed the execution of the ICC's decision, which had been issued on May 26, 2014, in favor of the Kazakhstani company, MGK LLP.[144] This delay underscores the complexities and potential challenges faced by foreign investors seeking the enforcement of arbitration awards in Kazakhstan's domestic court system.

The stage of mineral exploration that the Kazakhstani company found itself led the court to conclude that a debt settlement requirement would immediately bankrupt the company.[145] The Supreme Court also supported the First Instance Court's decision that the commercial discovery assessment's exploration period would be extended two years until 2016.[146] It also concluded that the ICC did not specify the period of execution of its decision.[147] However, this decision violated the Korean company's duty to keep the subsoil use rights as a joint investor.[148] Unlike the Kazakh state courts, the AIFC Court has no strict statutory deadlines for considering cases with strict timelines.[149] The Court aims to hear the case without times restrictions and to devote enough time for consideration of complex cases.[150]

Selecting the AIFC Court benefits oil and gas investors by eliminating the risk of unenforceable arbitration awards that can occur in Kazakhstan's national

---

[144] *See Resolution (ПОСТАНОВЛЕНИЕ), No.* 3гп-704-15, at 3–4 (2015), https://www2.deloitte.com/content/dam/Deloitte/kz/Documents/legal/Downloads/%D0%9A%D0%97_%D0%9F%D0%BE%D1%81%D1%82%D0%B0%D0%BD%D0%BE%D0%B2%D0%BB%D0%B5%D0%BD%D0%B8%D0%B5_Seha_Corporation.pdf.

[145] "..the demand for immediate repayment of the debt will lead to the bankrupty of the enterprise of the subsoil user who discovered minerals during the exploration period." (original text: "..требование немедленного погашения долга приведет к банкротству предприятия недропользователя, совершившего обнаружение полезных ископаемых в период разведки.") *Id.* at 4.

[146] *See id.* at 13.

[147] *See LT in Focus: Litigation Tracking*, DELOITTE (2016), at 13, https://www2.deloitte.com/content/dam/Deloitte/kz/Documents/legal/Downloads/KZ_Litigation%20Tracking_In%20Focus_eng.pdf.

[148] *Id. at* 13–14.

[149] REGULATIONS ON AIFC ACTS, AIFC REGULATIONS NO. 1 OF 2017 (Dec. 20, 2017, Astana, Kazakhstan). Bakhyt Tukulov, *On the Court and Arbitration at the Astana International Financial Center*, CHAMBERS AND PARTNERS (Nov. 18, 2018), https://chambers.com/articles/on-the-court-and-arbitration-at-the-astana-international-financial-center.

[150] *Id.*

courts.[151] The AIFC Court ensures that awards made under its rules, even if the arbitration takes place in different cities, are enforceable in Kazakhstan.[152] This provides a reliable and predictable mechanism for investors to secure the enforcement of arbitration decisions. For this reason, the parties entering to oil and gas industry agreements should ensure that they are members of the AIFC.

The AIFC Court has established a framework for enforcing IAC Arbitration Awards, Orders, and Judgments within the territorial jurisdiction of Kazakhstan.[153] To avail themselves of the AIFC Court's jurisdiction, parties must affiliate with the AIFC and conduct their contractual activities in conformity with the AIFC Rules.[154] In this regard, parties must explicitly stipulate the inclusion of the AIFC Court and IAC within the arbitration clause of their contracts or agreements prior to embarking on any contractual operations.[155] An illustrative case serves as a crucial reference point for comprehending the principles governing jurisdiction within the AIFC.

In *Modtech Group Teknoloji Sistemler LTD*,[156] the Court held that the parties had no jurisdiction under the AIFC Court based on Article 26(1)(b).[157] Under Article 26(1)(b), a dispute must relate to "operations carried out in the AIFC and regulated by the law of the AIFC."[158] The contract between the parties had no explicit connection with the AIFC, operations were not carried out in the AIFC and consequently were not regulated in the framework of the AIFC law.[159] The claimant, Modtech, was duly registered in the AIFC.[160] The primary respondent, Mosston Engineering LTD, was registered within the jurisdiction of the Seychelles, while Kaztechnology JSC operated under the legal framework of Kazakhstan.[161] The fourth company, "Fameway," although not directly involved in the ongoing legal proceedings, played a significant role in the AIFC Court's

---

[151] *See id.*
[152] *Id.*
[153] *See Rules on Arbitration and Mediation at the International Arbitration Centre*, Astana 2022 (IAC Rules), Art. 7, AIFC (Nov. 12, 2023), https://aifc.kz/files/legals/75/file/iac-rules-no-cover.pdf.
[154] *Id.*
[155] *Id.* arts. 6, 7.
[156]*See* Modtech Group Teknoloji Sistemleri Ltd v. Mosston Engineering Ltd and Kaztechnology Jsc, No. AIFC-C/CFI/2020/0010, (AIFC Feb. 21, 2022) (Justice of the Court: Justice Sir Stephen Richards (Kazakhstan)).
[157] *See id.*
[158] *Id.* ¶ 34.
[159] *Id.* ¶ 35.
[160] *Id.* ¶ 3(1).
[161] *Id.* ¶ 3(2), 3(3).

determination of non-jurisdiction.[162] Specifically, the crux of the matter revolved around two contracts involving Fameway and the two respondent companies—in this case, Mosston and Kaztechnology.[163] The initial contract, numbered 7/15 and dated April 2, 2015, pertained to a transaction between Kaztechnology, acting as the seller, and Mosston, as the buyer, with all three companies—Fameway, Kaztechnology, and Mosston—serving as participants in this contractual arrangement.[164] Contract 7/15 contained an arbitration provision.[165] The second contract, No. 15/45, where Mosston agreed to sell products to Fameway, did not contain provisions on dispute resolution.[166] Further, the Assignment Agreement concluded between the Claimant did not include a provision on the arbitration or dispute resolution, and the claim did not relate to the Assignment Agreement.[167] Since the dispute was raised in connection with Contract 7/15 and Contract 15/45 the AIFC Court concluded that Fameway had to file a claim against Mosston and Kaztechnology in order to find jurisdiction of the AIFC, and not under the Assignment Agreement.[168]

In another case in the AIFC, *Success K LLP*,[169] the parties submitted mirror image claims against each other based on the AIFC arbitration clause in their contracts.[170] The Claimant Success K LLP applied for recognition and enforcement of the Final Award against the Ministry of Health of Kazakhstan and the Ministry applied for annulment of this award in the AIFC Court.[171] The AIFC Court refused the Ministry's claim and ordered the enforcement of the final award.[172] This case illustrates that when the parties are members of the AIFC and included a reference to the rules in their contracts, the system in force in Kazakhstan may be highly efficient.

On the other hand, explicit rules that make it mandatory to carry out court decisions within Kazakhstan necessitate the creation of procedures for enforcing those decisions beyond the borders of Kazakhstan. Although the AIFC Court

---

[162] *Id.* ¶ 3(4).
[163] *Id.* ¶ 4, 4(1), 4(2).
[164] *Id.* ¶ 4(1).
[165] *Id.* ¶ 38.
[166] *Id.* ¶ 4(2); 38.
[167] *Id.* ¶ 38.
[168] *Id.* ¶ 36.
[169] *See* (1) Success K LLP v Ministry of Healthcare of the Republic of Kazakhstan, and (2) Ministry of Healthcare of the Republic of Kazakhstan v Success K LLP, No. AIFC-C/CFI/2021/0008 (AIFC Jan. 24, 2022) (Chief Justice of the Court: The Rt. Hon. The Lord Mance (Kazakhstan)).
[170] *Id.* ¶ 2.
[171] *Id.* ¶ 1.
[172] *See id.* ¶ 41.

Rules offer guidelines for enforcing judgments outside of Kazakhstan, there is currently no publicly available data on how effectively the AIFC Court enforces its decisions and orders in other countries.[173] Kazakhstan recognizes the enforcement of orders issued by the AIFC Court under the law titled "On Enforcement Proceeding and Court Bailiffs Status," No. 261-V dated April 2, 2010.[174] Accordingly, Article 30.11 of the AIFC Court Rules states that "any party seeking to enforce a judgment or order of the Court outside the Republic of Kazakhstan may apply for a certified copy of the judgment or order to be issued by the Court."[175]

The AIFC Court specifically includes that it has enforcement capabilities under the Minsk (1993) and Kiev (1992) Conventions for Central Asia countries;[176] including signatories such as Azerbaijan, China, Georgia, India, Kyrgyzstan, Uzbekistan, Lithuania, North Korea, Pakistan, Turkey, Turkmenistan, and UAE.[177] Further, Kazakhstan has a Court order agreement on enforcement at the bilateral level and maintains court-to-court reciprocity with several countries.[178]

6. CONCLUSION

It is my observation that based on the years of treaties and agreements that have concluded, the AIFC Court provisions are underutilized. Due to the AIFC's independent status from the Kazakhstan national court system, a potential concern arises regarding enforcement of AIFC Court decisions in foreign countries that maintain international treaties and agreements with Kazakhstan. For example, the Court of Dubai International Financial Center ("DIFC") also faced obstacles like enforcing its decisions outside of the UAE.[179] As a solution to this issue, the DIFC

---

[173] *Judgments & Orders 2019 - 2022 (Main)*, AIFC, https://court.aifc.kz/judgments/ (last accessed Dec. 6, 2022).

[174] Asem B. Bakenova, *AIFC Court as your dispute resolution forum: What you need to know*, MORGAN LEWIS (Jan. 26, 2022), https://www.morganlewis.com/pubs/2022/01/aifc-court-as-your-dispute-resolution-forum-what-you-need-to-know (last accessed Mar. 18, 2024).

[175] AIFC Court Rules, Art.30.11 (2018), https://aifc.kz/files/legals/69/file/3.-legislation-aifc-court-rules-2018.pdf.

[176] *Enforcement*, AIFC, https://court.aifc.kz/enforcement/ (last visited Dec. 6, 2022).

[177] *Id.*

[178] *Id.*

[179] *See AIFC Court As Your Dispute Resolution Forum: What You Need To Know*, MORGAN LEWIS (Jan. 26, 2022), https://www.morganlewis.com/pubs/2022/01/aifc-court-as-your-dispute-resolution-forum-what-you-need-to-know.

Court signed a memorandum with other countries' courts such as the Australia Federal Court,[180] the UK (Queen's Bench Division, England and Wales) Commercial Court,[181] and the Supreme Court of Singapore.[182] The DIFC also carries out memorandums and protocols with investment centers, universities, and other relevant entities to improve its effectiveness as an independent center of dispute resolution.[183] Following this example, concluding memorandums and protocols with extraterritorial courts may solve the problem of enforcing AIFC decisions outside of Kazakhstan.

The AIFC Court and IAC will be an advantageous forum for foreign investors wishing to invest in Kazakhstan's oil and gas industry. While the AIFC is a relatively recent establishment in Kazakhstan, separate from the national court system, the awards issued by AIFC Arbitration are expected to receive favorable treatment when it comes to recognition and enforcement by the AIFC Court within Kazakhstan. In addition, it will have advantages for disputes with large capital in controversy. To have jurisdiction under the AIFC, contracts must include the AIFC Court and the IAC in the arbitration clauses when foreign investors enter into contracts with members of the Kazakhstan oil and gas industry. Though uncertainties remain regarding the interpretation of AIFC legislation and jurisprudence, relevant practices are still developing. A successful track record of the enforcement of awards in Kazakhstan may persuade foreign investors from the oil and gas industry to include the AIFC arbitration clause in their agreements.

---

[180] *See* Memorandum on Guidance Between the Federal Court of Australia and DIFC Courts (Mar. 28, 2014) (on file with author).

[181] *See* Memorandum on Guidance as to Enforcement between the DIFC Courts and the Commercial Court (Jan. 23, 2013) (on file with author).

[182] *See* Memorandum on Understanding Between the Supreme Court of Singapore & DIFC Courts on References of Questions of Law (Jan. 19, 2022) (on file with author).

[183] *See Protocols & Memoranda*, DIFC COURTS, www.difccourts.ae/about/protocols-memoranda?ccm_paging_p=1&ccm_order_by=ak_date&ccm_order_by_direction=desc (last visited Dec. 6, 2022).

WILL EUROPEAN WITHDRAWAL FROM THE ENERGY CHARTER TREATY BE A SETBACK FOR INVESTMENTS IN THE REGION? THE FUTURE OF INVESTMENT ARBITRATION IN EUROPE AND REMEDIES FOR A POTENTIAL CRISIS OF JUSTICE

WERONIKA RYDZIŃSKA[*]

ABSTRACT

On November 24, 2022, the European Parliament adopted a resolution, by 303 votes to 209 with 63 abstentions, calling for a withdrawal from the Energy Charter Treaty ("ECT") by the European Union ("EU") and its Member States (so-called "European Withdrawal"). The EU's exit from the ECT is now unavoidable. This has put investors in a difficult position, and the further existence of investment arbitration has raised questions in Europe. Not only do investors have less time to claim protection for their investments, but they also have little time to invest in new investment projects that may be protected in Europe in the future.

The consequences of the European Withdrawal may be serious. As a result, a future economic development downturn in Europe may be observed. The lack of legal stability does not encourage foreign investors to invest in new energy projects in the region.

The European Commission has tentatively prepared exit proposals, but these may not be sufficient. The drafting process may take many years, during which investors in Europe will be left alone. The EU and Member States' laws provide less protection for investors.

What are the instant solutions for investors? Those who have made unsuccessful investments in the past can pursue their claims with the support of litigation financing mechanisms. Those who want to invest in energy projects in Europe will have to think creatively about the company's corporate structure.

Now, it is a sensible time for investors and EU states to consider how foreign energy investments might be governed in a potential ECT lacuna.

This paper examines the impact of the European Withdrawal and potential remedies for any consequences it may have in the near future. It is organized as follows.

The first chapter presents the basic information regarding the European Withdrawal, covering the European Commission's reasoning. The second chapter examines the impact of the European Withdrawal on investment arbitration. The analysis covers social, legal, and economic implications.

The third chapter analyzes potential gap fillers within the international, regional, and domestic legal frameworks. It examines specific international treaties, as well as European and local law in the context of the protection of foreign energy investments. The analysis also includes the legal instruments proposed by the European Commission.

The fourth chapter presents practical and instant remedies for investors to overcome the difficult situation they face in Europe with the protection of their investments. It refers to the financing of their claim via litigation finance and to the corporate structure mechanisms that investors may implement to protect their investments in Europe.

The final chapter assesses the situation that investors will face after the European Withdrawal and concludes that the coming months or even years may not be easy for the EU, but is also difficult for the investors.

Keywords: investment arbitration, ECT, third – party funding, European Union, EU law, international law

*LL.M Candidate at University Torino (Italy)/WIPO, Lawyer/Advocate, MA Law at Cardinal Stefan Wyszynski University in Warsaw, Poland; Contact: weronika.rydzinska@gmail.com

1.	*EUROPEAN WITHDRAWAL FROM THE ENERGY CHARTER TREATY*	*67*
2.	*RESULTS OF THE EUROPEAN WITHDRAWAL*	*74*
A.	Legal Implications	76
B.	Social and Economic Implications	82
3.	*HOW TO FIX THE EUROPEAN WITHDRAWAL? LEGISLATION GAP FILLERS FOR INVESTORS*	*84*
A.	International Regulation	85
B.	Regional Regulations	88
C.	Multilateral Investment Court ("MCT")	90
D.	Domestic Regulations	91
4.	*WHAT CAN INVESTORS DO?*	*93*
5.	*CONCLUSIONS*	*95*

1. EUROPEAN WITHDRAWAL FROM THE ENERGY CHARTER TREATY

November 24, 2022 was a day that made history in Europe and worldwide. On that day, the European Parliament, by 303 votes to 209, with 63 abstentions, adopted a resolution calling on the European Union ("EU") and its Member States to withdraw from the Energy Charter Treaty ("ECT") (the so-called "European Withdrawal").[1] The ECT has been criticized for blocking efforts to fight climate change because its protection of energy investments extends to fossil fuels.[2] This led to serious changes in the European energy market.

On July 7, 2023, the European Commission has proposed that the EU and its Member States withdraw, in a coordinated manner, from the ECT.[3] It was possible under Article 47 of the ECT.[4] EU Energy Commissioner Kadri Simson stated that, "I proposed that the EU withdraws from the Energy Charter Treaty, because in its current, unmodernized version it is no longer in line with the European Union's energy and climate goals."[5] A coordinated withdrawal from the ECT, now supported by the European Commission, would have the EU, Euratom, and all EU Member States leave the treaty. This accord also counts more than 20 states outside the EU among its contracting parties.[6] However, it seems that the European states are divided. Countries including Cyprus, Hungary, and Slovakia were first skeptical of withdrawing from the ECT and "said they would prefer to stay in an updated version of the accord."[7] Nevertheless, the withdrawal of the EU

---

[1] European Parliament resolution on the outcome of the modernization of the Energy Charter Treaty (2022/2934(RSP)), Nov. 22, 2022, O.J. (L167) 18.

[2] Kate Abnett, *EU Proposes Energy Charter Treaty Exit After Climate Concerns*, Thomson Reuters, Jul. 7, 2023, at 2, https://www.reuters.com/sustainability/climate-energy/eu-proposes-energy-charter-treaty-exit-after-climate-concerns-2023-07-07/.

[3] Comm'n Decision Withdrawing the Proposal for a Council Decision on the position to be taken on behalf of Euratom in the 33rd meeting of the Energy Charter Conference, COM (2022)/C-522, Jul. 7, 2023.

[4] The Energy Charter Treaty, art. 47, Dec. 17, 1994, 100 L.N.T.S. 137.

[5] Federica Di Sario, *EU Moves To Quit Energy Investment Treat*, POLITICO (Jul. 7, 2023), https://www.politico.eu/article/energy-charter-treaty-ect-investment-europe-quit/.

[6] Lukas Schaugg et. al., *United We Leave or Divided We Stay? Why it's time for the EU to speak with one voice regarding the Energy Charter Treaty*, INT'L INST. FOR SUSTAINABLE DEVELOPMENT (Jul. 20, 2023), https://www.iisd.org/articles/deep-dive/united-we-leave-divided-we-stay-energy-charter-treaty.

[7] *EU proposes Energy Charter Treaty exit after climate concerns*, THOMSON REUTERS (July 7, 2023), https://www.reuters.com/sustainability/climate-energy/eu-proposes-energy-charter-treaty-exit-after-climate-concerns-2023-07-07/; Di Sario, *supra* note 5, at 49.

from the ECT is now inevitable.

The European Withdrawal has a relative impact on investors in Europe – their future investments will not be protected, and the protection of current investments will be limited. Some investors may thus abandon investments in the region they have been planning for a long time, which could have repercussions on the global economy.

The European energy market consists of open and competitive energy markets in the member states.[8] It aims to create new economic opportunities and increase the level of cross-border trade to achieve higher efficiency and better quality of service, as well as to ensure security of supply.[9] The development of the internal energy market is important because of possible price reductions, as energy costs account for a significant portion of variable costs in many industries.[10] Consequently, the energy market remains crucial to the global economy.

One of the main legal acts within the European energy market was the ECT – a legal agreement with international status, consisting of various provisions for the interaction of its signatories on energy issues.[11] The ECT exclusively regulates cooperation in the energy sector.[12] As the world's largest multilateral treaty, it is a heavily scrutinized international investment agreement ("IIA") and one that is subject to ongoing modernization efforts.[13] Before proceeding any further, it is worth mentioning the history of its creation until after the modernization procedure.

This ECT was signed in 1994 (entered into force in 1998), providing an international framework for energy cooperation.[14] Its purpose is to promote energy security while ensuring support for investors in the host country.[15] It

---

[8] Int'l Energy Charter, The Energy Charter Treaty [1994], Int'l Energy Charter (Feb. 18, 2019), at 2, https://www.energycharter.org/process/energy-charter-treaty-1994/energy-charter-treaty/.
[9] Magdalena Jaś-Nowopolska, *The Influence of the Energy Charter Treaty on the European Energy market*, 4 INT'L COMP. JURIS. 77, 78 (2018).
[10] *Id.*
[11] The Energy Charter Treaty, Dec. 17, 1994, 100 L.N.T.S. 137.
[12] Agata Daszko, *No Longer Feeling the Energy: Unpacking Poland's reasoning behind its decision to withdraw from the ECT*, VERFBLOG (Sept. 9, 2022), https://verfassungsblog.de/not-feeling-the-energy-anymore/.
[13] *Id.*
[14] The Energy Charter Treaty, Dec. 17, 1994, 100 L.N.T.S. 137.
[15] Gaïa Bottoni, et. al, *The Union Shall End Protection of Investments in Fossil Fuels in The Context of the Modernisation of the Energy Charter Treaty (European Parliament, 2020)*, GENERATION CLIMATE EUROPE, https://gceurope.org/the-ect-an-obstacle-to-the-energy-transition-how-did-we-

addresses many aspects of the energy sector, from the investment regime to the definition of energy products and equipment, and also reaches into environmental issues.[16] It also resulted from the need to strengthen cooperation between the rich West and the poorer Eastern Bloc countries in the 1990s.[17] The first to put forward this vision was Ruud Lubbers, the prime minister of the Netherlands.[18]

The four pillars of the ECT are: the protection of foreign investments, the existence of non-discriminatory conditions, the resolution of investment disputes between the investor and state, and the promotion of energy efficiency in an attempt to mitigate the negative environmental impact of energy production and use.[19] The protection of investments covers the basic international rules such as: fair and equitable treatment, non-discriminatory provisions, umbrella clause, and most favored nation clause.[20] One of the most important rules under each international investment dispute is the protection against expropriation.[21]

ECT currently has 50 signatories[22] as the number of members has been decreasing in recent years despite the modernization process. Following the wave of ECT arbitration proceedings against various EU Member States, including Spain, Italy, and the Czech Republic, in the mid-2010s, the European Commission

---

get-here/ (last visited Apr. 19, 2024).

[16] *Id.*

[17] *Id.*

[18] *See* RAFAEL LEAL-ARCAS, COMMENTARY ON THE ENERGY CHARTER TREATY 2 (Edward Elgar Publishing, 2d. ed., 2023), https://www.elgaronline.com/view/edcoll/9781788117487/9781788117487.xml.

[19] Kaj Hobér, *Investment Arbitration and the Energy Charter Treaty*, 1 J. INT'L DISP. SETTLEMENT 153–90 (2010).

[20] OECD, Fair and Equitable Treatment Standard in International Investment Law, OECD Working Papers on International Investment, 2004/03, (2004), OECD Publishing. http://dx.doi.org/10.1787/675702255435.

[21] Derek Soller et al., *Substantive Protections: Expropriation*, GLOB. ARB. REV. (Dec. 21, 2023) (citing Energy Charter Treaty, Article 13(1); Treaty between United States of America and the Argentine Republic Concerning the Reciprocal Encouragement and Protection of Investment, Article V; Agreement on encouragement and reciprocal protection of investments between the Kingdom of the Netherlands and the Republic of Venezuela, Article VI. https://globalarbitrationreview.com/guide/the-guide-investment-treaty-protection-and-enforcement/second-edition/article/substantive-protections-expropriation#footnote-095).

[22] The Energy Charter Treaty, Dec. 17, 1994, 100 L.N.T.S. 137; *Contracting Parties and Signatories of the Energy Charter Treaty*, INT'L ENERGY CHARTER, *https://www.energychartertreaty.org/treaty/contracting-parties-and-signatories/* (last visited Apr. 20, 2024).

started voicing its dissatisfaction with the ECT and calling for reform.[23] Starting October, 2022,[24] ten EU countries announced or notified the denunciation of the treaty.

In 2011, the European Commission explicitly advocated for a need to extend the ECT's geographical coverage without changing its content.[25] The European Commission led the modernization process principally to align the ECT with the Paris Agreement.[26] The EU's policy stance changed in 2018, more than a year before the adoption of the EU Green Deal,[27] a framework document announced in December 2019 to achieve Europe's climate neutrality by 2050. In the document, the European Commission stated, among other things, that "[t]he ECT's investment protection provisions have not been updated since the 1990s and are now outdated compared to the new standards of the EU's reformed approach to investment policy."[28] Recently, the anti-EU declarations have been presented by France, Luxembourg, and Spain.[29] Mounting pressure by European civil society has brought to light the ECT's shortcomings and inconsistency with EU policies,[30] calling on the European Commission to take action by seizing the

---

[23] Nicholas Lawn et.al., *The End Is Near: The European Commission's Proposed Coordinated Withdrawal from the ECT*, KLUWER ARB. BLOG 13 (Jul. 24, 2023), https://arbitrationblog.kluwerarbitration.com/2023/07/24/the-end-is-near-the-european-commissions-proposed-coordinated-withdrawal-from-the-ect/.

[24] In October 2022 Spain and the Netherlands, and in November 2022, Slovenia and Luxemburg, expressed their intent to withdraw; On March 22, 2023, the Energy Charter Depositary confirmed that France, Germany and Poland had filed written notifications of withdrawal from the ECT; In April 2023, Denmark and in July 2023 Portugal, both announced the intention to withdraw.

[25] European Commission, *Communication to the European Parliament, the Council, the European Economic and Social Committee and the Committee of the Regions of 7 September 2011 on security of energy supply and international cooperation – 'The EU Energy Policy: Engaging with Partners Beyond Our Borders*, COM (2011) 539 final, 9–14.

[26] Paris Agreement to the United Nations Framework Convention on Climate Change, Dec. 12, 2015, T.I.A.S. No. 16-1104 (hereinafter *Paris Agreement*).

[27] *Communication from the Commission to the European Parliament, the European Council, the Council, the European Economic and Social Committee of the Regions,* The European Green Deal, COM(2019)640 final.

[28] European Commission, Newsletter, *Commission presents EU proposal for modernizing Energy Charter Treaty* (May 27, 2020), https://policy.trade.ec.europa.eu/news/commission-presents-eu-proposal-modernising-energy-charter-treaty-2020-05-27_en.

[29] Kingdom of Spain, *Letter to the European Commission Vice-President Franz Timmermans* (Feb. 9, 2021).

[30] Fabian Flues, et al., *Busting the Myths Around the Energy Charter Treaty: A Guide for Concerned Citizens, Activists, Journalists and Policymakers,* Berlin,

momentum of the ECT's ongoing renegotiation—or "modernization."[31]

The ECT's modernization process also includes consolidation, expansion, and outreach, i.e., the Consolidation, Expansion, and Outreach ("CONEXO") policy, launched in 2012.[32] The CONEXO policy aims/strives for intergovernmental cooperation, activities, and reports produced for targeted countries,[33] along with the International Energy Charter Declaration, a political declaration reflecting modern energy challenges.[34] However, none of these initiatives have been transformed into binding legislation.

The process of renegotiating the ECT took place fifteen times (the last time on June 23, 2022)[35] and concluded during the Ad Hoc Meeting of the Energy Charter Conference, June 24, 2022. Finalization,[36] when the contracting parties reached an Agreement in Principle, which, among other reforms, includes significantly narrower standards of protection, more limited definitions of "investor" and "investment," a mechanism for early dismissal of frivolous claims, and a provision on the right to regulate, including in relation to climate change mitigation and adaptation.[37]

The reformed ECT continues to protect both the existing and new investments in fossil fuels, but not for investments within the EU and the United

---

Brussels, and Amsterdam: PowerShift, CORPORATE EUROPE OBSERVATORY, AND TRANSNATIONAL INSTITUTE (Dec. 2020), https://www.tni.org/files/publication-downloads/busting_the_myths_around_the_energy_charter_treaty-web.pdf.

[31] Martin Dietrich Brauch, *Modernizing the Energy Charter Treaty: A Make-or-Break Moment for Sustainable, Climate-Friendly Energy Policy*, INTERNATIONAL INSTITUTE FOR SUSTAINABLE DEVELOPMENT ("IISD") (Nov. 13, 2019), https://www.iisd.org/articles/modernizing-energy-charter-treaty-make-or-break-moment-sustainable-climate-friendly-energy.

[32] Energy Charter Secretariat, *Decision of the Energy Charter Conference, Road Map for the Modernisation of the Energy Charter Process*, CCDEC 2010, 10 GEN.

[33] Energy Charter Secretariat, *Decision of the Energy Charter Conference, Policy on Outreach, Expansion and Consolidation - Report by the Secretary General*, CCDEC 2011, 2 NOT.

[34] Concluding Document of the Ministerial ("The Hague II") Conference on the International Energy Charter, introduced in 2015.

[35] International Energy Charter Secretariat, *Modernization of the Treaty* (Feb. 12, 2021), https://www.energychartertreaty.org/modernisation-of-the-treaty.

[36] Energy Charter Secretariat, *Decision of the Energy Charter Conference* (June 24, 2022), https://www.energycharter.org/fileadmin/DocumentsMedia/CCDECS/2022/CCDEC202210.pdf.

[37] *Id.*

Kingdom ("UK").³⁸ Any investments made after August 15, 2023 are no longer protected (those before will be protected, at the latest, until the end of 2040).³⁹ However, there are exceptions for certain gas-related investments in power plants, infrastructure, and pipelines, which would remain protected until the end of 2030 or, at the latest, until the end of 2040.⁴⁰ Japan, Switzerland, and Turkey have opted to apply the flexibility mechanism to EU (and UK) investors on a reciprocal basis.⁴¹ These countries, therefore, have unchanged investor protection.⁴² The remaining ECT signatories reached a compromise between the EU's rationale, which, more than most investment treaties, is consistent with the Green Deal assumptions.⁴³ However, several EU Member States announced their intention to withdraw from the ECT a few weeks before the Agreement in Principle was to be adopted.⁴⁴ Some scholars claim that the content of the introduced modifications and changes to the ECT, which are inconsistent with the EU's new approaches, dictate the EU's decision.⁴⁵

Meanwhile, in Komstroy, the Court of Justice of the EU ("CJEU") reasoned that investment disputes between an EU member state and an investor from another EU member state are to be declared incompatible with EU law and held that Article 26(2)(c) ECT must be interpreted as not being applicable to disputes between a Member State and an investor of another Member State concerning an investment made by the latter in the first Member State.⁴⁶ Therefore, the CJEU's

---

³⁸ Agreement in Principle, Annex NI, Section B, Article 1, https://www.bilaterals.org/IMG/pdf/reformed_ect_text.pdf [hereinafter *Annex NI, Section B, Article 1*].
³⁹ Agreement in Principle, Annex NI, Section C, Article 1, https://www.bilaterals.org/IMG/pdf/reformed_ect_text.pdf.
⁴⁰ Annex NI, Section B, Article 1, *supra* note 38.
⁴¹ Agreement in Principle, Annex NPT and Annex IA-NI, https://www.bilaterals.org/IMG/pdf/reformed_ect_text.pdf.
⁴² *Id.*
⁴³ *Id.*
⁴⁴ *Written notifications of withdrawal from the Energy Charter Treaty*, INTERNATIONAL ENERGY CHARTER (Mar. 22, 2023), https://www.energycharter.org/media/news/article/written-notifications-of-withdrawal-from-the-energy-charter-treaty/.
⁴⁵ Martin Dietrich Brauch, *Should the European Union Fix, Leave or Kill the Energy Charter Treaty?*, COLUMBIA CENTER ON SUSTAINABLE INVESTMENT (Feb. 9, 2023), https://blogdroiteuropeen.com/2021/02/09/should-the-european-union-fix-leave-or-kill-the-energy-charter-treaty-by-martin-dietrich-brauch.
⁴⁶ *Id.* Already in 2011, some commentators had highlighted the inevitable conclusion that, from the vantage point of EU law, a cross-border investment between the EU Member States is not a "foreign" investment. See for example: Christer Söderlund, *The Future of the Energy Charter Treaty in the context of the*

court decision implies that intra-EU arbitration under the ECT breaches EU law in its current form. The CJEU justified the normative autonomy of EU law "by the essential characteristics of the EU and its law, relating to the constitutional structure of the European Union and the very nature of that law."[47]

Consequently, the European Parliament adopted a resolution calling on the Commission to prepare a coordinated withdrawal of the EU and its Member States.[48] In response, the Energy Charter Secretariat sent a letter pointing out some misunderstandings in the Parliament's resolution and stressing that the EU should continue to support the adoption of a modernized Energy Charter Treaty, even if it later intends to withdraw from it.[49] As a next step in the European Withdrawal process, the European Commission issued a "non-paper" in which the three solutions were presented, including the coordinated withdrawal by the EU and its Member States (jointly).[50]

In the modernization process, Member states also attempted to undermine the modernization process. For example, Belgium requested an opinion from the CJEU on the modernized ECT.[51] On June 16, 2022, the CJEU published Opinion 1/20, concluding that Belgium's request for an opinion on the draft modernized ECT compatibility with EU law was inadmissible.[52]

Finally, on July 7, 2023 (i.e., 6 months after the EU proposal on modernization of the ECT failed to be adopted), the European Communities made a declaration under ECT Article 25 which establishes a carve-out from the ECT

Lisbon Treaty, Graham Coop (ed.); *Energy Dispute Resolution: Investment Protection, Transit and the Energy Charter Treaty*, JURISNET 106 (2011).

[47] Brauch, *supra* note 45.

[48] Resolution of the European Parliament of Nov. 24, 2022 on the outcome of the modernisation of the Energy Charter Treaty (2022/2934 (RSP)).

[49] Letter of the International Energy Charter Secretary General to Ms. Roberta Metsola, President of the European Parliament (Feb. 13, 2023), SG/23/E/0047.

[50] European Commission, *Non-paper from the European Commission. Next steps as regards the EU, Euroatom and Member States' membership in the Energy Charter Treaty*, ENERGY CHARTER CONFERENCE (Nov. 22, 2022), https://www.euractiv.com/wp-content/uploads/sites/2/2023/02/Non-paper_ECT_nextsteps.pdf (last visited Jan. 7, 2024).

[51] *Belgium Requests an Opinion on the Intra-European Application of the Arbitration Provisions of the Future Modernised Energy Charter Treaty*, Kingdom of Belgium, Foreign Affairs, Foreign Trade and Development Cooperation (website), Kingdom of Belgium, Foreign Affairs, Foreign Trade and Development Cooperation, (Dec. 3, 2020).

[52] Opinion 1/20 of the Court (Fourth Chamber) (Opinion pursuant to Article 218(11) TFEU – Request for an Opinion – Draft modernized Energy Charter Treaty – Article 26 – Dispute settlement mechanism – Admissibility) (June 16, 2022).

in that it allows the extension of EU law benefits between the Member States to the extent that these rules are more favorable for investors.[53] It does not shield respondent states from obligations under the ECT if the rules under the ECT are more favorable for investors.[54] In response, the Secretary General of the ECT Secretariat issued a press release expressing his "profound regret" and appealing to all EU Member States to support the modernized ECT, regardless of whether they intended to withdraw.[55]

The whole world should actively watch further legal and political developments related to the Treaty. This is all the more so as the EU does not appear to be prepared for the end of the Treaty. International, regional, and national law lack complete legal solutions to provide investors with a sense of security. The European Withdrawal will have legal and social consequences and may also affect the global economy (*inter alia*, due to a reduction in foreign investment).

2. RESULTS OF THE EUROPEAN WITHDRAWAL

Discussions between the Commission and Member States take place behind closed doors, and it is impossible to determine what the motivations for the European Withdrawal of individuals from the EU member states are. Some may argue that a compelling argument arises from the legislative endeavors of the EU aimed at promoting renewable energy, particularly concerning the divestment of investments in fossil fuels. However, Jason Bordoff underlined that it "does not make sense unless a sharp change in the energy demand structure is achieved."[56] Hence, action taken by one economy in the world may not be enough, and appropriate action should be taken globally for such 'sharp change' to occur.

The other reason for the European Withdrawal might be that the ECT treats international investors inequitably favorably compared to ordinary persons or

---

[53] Directorate-General for Energy, *European Commission proposes a coordinated EU withdrawal from the Energy Charter Treaty*, EUROPEAN COMMISSION (July 7, 2023).

[54] Prof. Dr. Christina Eckes, Dr. Laurens Ankersmit, *The Compatibility of the Energy Charter Treaty with EU law*, UNIVERSITY OF AMSTERDAM, AMSTERDAM CENTRE FOR EUROPEAN LAW AND GOVERNANCE 4, 20 (Apr. 21, 2022).

[55] *Statement by the Secretary General of the Energy Charter Secretariat on the draft Council Decision proposing the withdrawal of the European Union from the Energy Charter Treaty*, INTERNATIONAL ENERGY CHARTER (July 11, 2023), https://www.energycharter.org/media/news/article/statement-by-the-secretary-general-of-the-energy-charter-secretariat-on-the-draft-council-decision-p/.

[56] Andrei Belyi, *The Energy Charter process in the face of uncertainties*, 14 J. WORLD ENERGY L. & BUS. 363–75 (Sept. 2021).

national investors. Article 16 of the ECT illustrates this point.⁵⁷ It states:

> Where two or more Contracting Parties have entered into a prior international agreement, or enter into a subsequent international agreement, whose terms in either case concern . . . this Treaty, . . . nothing in such terms of the other agreement shall be construed to derogate from . . . this Treaty or from any right to dispute resolution with respect thereto under this Treaty, where any such provision is more favourable to the Investor or Investment.⁵⁸

Hence, this argument should be disregarded since it is clear that nationals are treated the same way as foreign investors.

Criticism of the treaty on the grounds of inequality is much broader.⁵⁹ The United Nations ("UN") Special Rapporteur, David R. Boyd in his report mentioned that "[f]oreign investors have armed themselves with a secret international arbitration process known as investor-state dispute settlement ("ISDS") . . . This unfair, undemocratic, and dysfunctional process has created a crisis of legitimacy in the international investment system."⁶⁰

In fact, however, the real reason for the dissatisfaction may have been something else entirely. Namely, for many years, EU Member States have been forced to pay the adjudicated claims in the investment arbitration to foreign

---

⁵⁷ The Energy Charter Treaty, art. 16, Dec. 17, 1994, 100 L.N.T.S. 137, https://www.energychartertreaty.org/provisions/part-iii-investment-promotion-and-protection/article-16-relation-to-other-agreements/. Energy Charter Treaty, Article 16: Relation to Other Agreements https://www.energychartertreaty.org/provisions/part-iii-investment-promotion-and-protection/article-16-relation-to-other-agreements/.

⁵⁸ *Id.*

⁵⁹ Nikki Reisch, *Investors v. Climate Action What recent case law and treaty reforms may mean for the future of investment arbitration in the energy sector*, CENTER FOR INTERNATIONAL ENVIRONMENTAL LAW (Sept. 2022), https://www.ciel.org/investors-v-climate-action/; *The EU must withdraw from the Energy Charter Treaty*, CLIENTEARTH (Sept. 20, 2022) https://www.clientearth.org/latest/latest-updates/news/the-eu-must-withdraw-from-the-energy-charter-treaty/.

⁶⁰ David R. Boyd, *Paying polluters: the catastrophic consequences of investor-State dispute settlement for climate and environment action and human rights*, 78 United Nations General Assembly (July 13, 2023) https://files.lbr.cloud/public/2023-11/Paying%20polluters%2C%20the%20catastrophic%20consequences%20of%20ISDS%20for%20climate%20and%20environment%20action%20and%20human%20rights_1.pdf?VersionId=o7acnXU2vI4FDuSy2fXsdwbjFyavkr3t.

investors seeking legal protection for their investments.[61] The argument is also primarily surprising given that in investment arbitration, as in ordinary courts, each chooses an arbitrator, has an equal opportunity to present its case, and can access an annulment system or otherwise challenge the award.[62] Although the reasons for the European Withdrawal are not entirely clear, the consequences for investors are evident.

While the consequences of the European Withdrawal will be borne mainly by the investors, society will also suffer. The investments made in the region have serious social and economic implications.[63] A comprehensive analysis of these effects is presented below.

A. Legal Implications

One of the serious consequences for investors in the EU is the limited legal protection, i.e., the 20-year sunset clause (provided by Article 47(3) of the ECT).[64]

Although some activists and political representatives are advocating the abolition of the sunset clause, it remains in force. As an example, Nathalie Bernasconi-Osterwalder of the International Institute for Sustainable Development suggested that investors sue treaty signatories in the event of a violation of investment protection.[65] Some scholars point out that even the mere threat of pursuing cases and guaranteeing investor protection can discourage governments from taking action on climate change.[66]

However, in its Proposal, the European Commission stated that the effects of the sunset clause would apply to intra-EU affairs (for the next twenty years), securing the protection mechanism for the investments made in the EU.[67] Despite

---

[61] *Disputes between foreign investors and EU governments*, EUR-LEX, https://eur-lex.europa.eu/EN/legal-content/summary/disputes-between-foreign-investors-and-eu-governments.html (last visited Mar. 31, 2024).

[62] Daria Davitti & Paolo Vargiu, *Litigation Finance and the Assetization of International Investment Arbitration*, 24 J. WORLD INV. & TR. 487, 493 (2023).

[63] Denis Bouget, Hugh Frazer, Eric Marlier, Sebastiano Sabato, Bart Vanhercke, *Social Investment in Europe: A study of national policies*, EUROPEAN COMMISSION (2015).

[64] The Energy Charter Treaty, art. 47(3), Dec. 17, 1994, 100 L.N.T.S. 137, https://www.energychartertreaty.org/provisions/part-iii-investment-promotion-and-protection/article-16-relation-to-other-agreements/.

[65] Andrei V. Belyi, *New Challenges to the Liberal World Order: Reassessing Controversies Surrounding the Energy Charter Treaty*, ICDS DIPLOMAATIA MAGAZINE (July 1, 2020).

[66] Kyla Tienhaara & Christian Downie, *Risky Business? The Energy Charter Treaty, Renewable Energy, and Investor-State Disputes*, 24 GLOBAL GOVERNANCE 451, 452 (July-Sept. 2018).

[67] *Proposal of the European Commission for a Council Decision on the*

the European Commission's clear stance in a draft inter se agreement regarding the non-application of the sunset clause to intra-EU relations,[68] during the modernization process several arbitral tribunals have consistently dismissed this position.[69] This criticism has been supported by Article 41(1)(b) of the Vienna Convention on the Law of Treaties ("VCLT"), which does not allow modifications of international agreements when they affect the enjoyment of rights by the parties to those agreements. The arbitral tribunals pointed out that the particular modification of the ECT proposed in the present case would be "prohibited by the treaty" contrary to Article 41(1)(b) of the VCLT, as Article 16(2) of the ECT expressly prevents the later treaty from being interpreted as a derogation from the "more favorable rights granted to investors in Parts III and V of the ECT."[70] Such rejection could potentially impact the future legal standing of investors. They may face situations where their legal position will be uncertain even after the award as arbitral tribunals may rule in a manner contrary to the views of EU and EU member state authorities, which will have an impact on the certainty of investors' rights.

The end of the twenty-year term assured by the sunset clause will result in various dispute resolution methods becoming obsolete. These include (1) arbitration between states (with specific procedures for competition and environmental issues), (2) dispute mechanisms based on the World Trade Organization ("WTO") for trade, (3) conciliation procedures for transit, (4) a new early warning system, and (5) the well-known and increasingly used investor-state

---

withdrawal of the Union from the Energy Charter Treaty, European Commission Brussels COM (2023) 447 final, p.3. (July 7, 2023).
[68] *Annex to the Communication from the Commission to the European Parliament and the Council, as well as to the Member States on an Agreement between the Member States, the European Union, and the European Atomic Energy Community on the Interpretation of the Energy Charter Treaty*, European Commission Brussels COM (2022) 523 final (Oct. 5, 2022), https://eur-lex.europa.eu/resource.html?uri=cellar:3d54cece-4494-11ed-92ed-01aa75ed71a1.0001.02/DOC_2&format=PDF (last visited Jan. 7, 2024).
[69] *See, e.g.* Vattenfall v. Germany, ICSID Case No. ARB/12/12, Decision on the Achmea Issue, August 31, 2018; Landesbank v Spain, ICSID Case No. ARB/15/45, Decision on the "Intra-EU" Jurisdictional Objection, February 25, 2019; Eskol v Italy, ICSID Case No. ARB/15/50, Decision on Italy's Request for Immediate Termination and Italy's Jurisdictional Objection based on Inapplicability of the ECT to Intra-EU Disputes, May 7, 2019.
[70] Vattenfall v. Germany, ICSID Case No. ARB/12/12, Decision on the Achmea Issue, August 31, 2018, para. 221; Eskol v Italy, ICSID Case No. ARB/15/50, Decision on Italy's Request for Immediate Termination and Italy's Jurisdictional Objection based on Inapplicability of the ECT to Intra-EU Disputes, May 7, 2019, para. 151.

dispute settlement ("ISDS") clause.[71] ISDS allows investors to sue states for infringements of their investments in an international forum.[72] Disputes are often presided over by panels of three arbitrators—one chosen by the state, one chosen by the investor, and the third mutually agreed on or appointed by an arbitral institution such as the International Centre for the Settlement of Investment Disputes ("ICSID") or Stockholm Chamber of Commerce ("SCC").[73]

The most litigious sector in ISDS worldwide is the fossil fuel industry, accounting for 20% of the total known ISDS cases across all sectors.[74] Some of the largest fossil fuel companies have been successful in ISDS with an award amounting to over 1 billion USD.[75] The company Rockhopper won an award of €190 million (plus interest) in compensation for the Italian government's decision to ban oil drilling in coastal areas out of environmental concerns.[76] In 2021, German Energy companies RWE and Uniper both lodged claims of €1.4 billion and €1 billion, respectively, against the Netherlands for prohibiting coal-fired power generation by 2030 to comply with the Paris Climate Agreement.[77] One more example is a UK-based energy company, Ascent Resources, which lodged a €500 million damages claim against Slovenia requiring an environmental impact assessment for the company's gas project with the help of low-volume hydraulic

---

[71] *See generally* Antonios Kouroutakis, *Sunset Clauses in International Law and their Consequences for EU Law,* Policy DEPARTMENT FOR CITIZENS' RIGHTS AND CONSTITUTIONAL AFFAIRS DIRECTORATE-GENERAL FOR INTERNAL POLICIES (2022), https://www.europarl.europa.eu/RegData/etudes/STUD/2022/703592/IPOL_STU(2022)703592_EN.pdf.
[72] *Primer on International Treaties and Investor-State Dispute Settlement*, COLUMBIA CENTER ON SUSTAINABLE INVESTMENT (Jan. 2022).
[73] The Energy Charter Treaty, art. 26, Dec. 17, 1994, 100 L.N.T.S. 137, https://www.energychartertreaty.org/provisions/part-iii-investment-promotion-and-protection/article-16-relation-to-other-agreements/.
[74] Bart-Jaap Verbeek, *The Modernization of the Energy Charter Treaty: Fulfilled or Broken Promises?*, 8 BUS. & HUMAN RIGHTS J. 97, 99 (2023).
[75] UNCTAD, *Investment Dispute Settlement Navigator*, https://investmentpolicy.unctad.org/investmentdispute-settlement (last accessed Jan. 7, 2024).
[76] *Oil Firm Rockhopper Wins Payout from Italian Government After Drilling Ban*, PINSENT MASONS LLP (Aug. 30, 2022), https://www.pinsentmasons.com/out-law/news/rockhopper-wins-italian-government-drilling-ban#:~:text=The%20oil%20firm%20Rockhopper%20has,offshore%20from%20Abruzzo%2C%20southern%20Italy.
[77] *RWE v. Netherlands*, ICSID Case No. ARB/21/4; *Uniper v. Netherlands*, ICSID Case No. ARB/21/22.

fracturing and the subsequent adoption of a hydraulic fracking ban.[78] Moreover, research from the International Institute for Sustainable Development ("IISD") in 2021 shows that arbitration claims challenging environmental measures, including climate measures, are on the rise.[79]

The Energy Charter Secretariat maintains an updated list of investment dispute settlement cases where, as of June 1, 2022, the total number of ECT cases was 150.[80] The first ECT case was registered in 2001.[81] Between 2011 and 2017, there was a boom in investment arbitration cases concerning renewable energy sources, and by 2020, more than half of cases concerned investment arbitration.[82] In terms of compensation, renewable-related awards amounted to "EUR 1 billion USD against EUR 503 million for fossil fuels," excluding the exceptional *Yukos* case.[83]

Thus, without the ECT, not only could investing without guarantees of respect for the rule of law carry much higher risks,[84] but EU member states have lost the multilateral treaty that protects energy investments and promotes the rule of law through strong investment incentives, including renewable energy sources projects. With widespread changes in Europe and the rule of law crisis (Poland in years 2018-2024, or Hungary),[85] European countries may face challenges

---

[78] *Ascent v Slovenia*, ICSID Case No. ARB/22/21.

[79] *Investor–State Disputes in the Fossil Fuel Industry*, International Institute for Sustainable Development, 2021, https://www.iisd.org/publications/report/investor-state-disputes-fossil-fuel-industry (last accessed Jan. 7, 2024).

[80] The list of cases is available at: https://www.energychartertreaty.org/cases/list-of-cases/ (last accessed Jan. 7, 2024).

[81] *Id.*; AES Summit Generation Limited v. Republic of Hungary, ICSID Case No. ARB/01/4.

[82] Fernando Dias Simoes, *When Green Incentives Go Pale: Investment Arbitration and Renewable Energy Policymaking*, 45 DENVER J. INT'L L. & POL'Y 251, 261 (2017).

[83] Andrei Belyi, *The Energy Charter Process in the Face of Uncertainties*, 14 J. WORLD ENERGY L. & BUS. 363, 371 (2021).

[84] *See e.g., Ascom Group S.A., Anatolie Stati, Gabriel Stati and Terra Raf Trans Traiding Ltd. v. Republic of Kazakhstan* (I), SCC Case No. 116/2010: (finding in a dispute over bonds of Tristan Oil company, including the rights of the bondholder, U.S. fund manager Argent Creek Partners, were violated by the Kazakh government, which orchestrated an illegal takeover of the company. In 2013, the arbitral panel ordered the Republic to pay over US$500 million in compensation and damages to Tristan Oil. To date, this amount has not been paid despite numerous judgments by state courts in Europe ordering enforcement of the award).

[85] William Schwartz, *Protecting the Rule of Law in Hungary and Poland*,

attracting foreign direct investment ("FDI"), which may have implications for the global economy. This topic will be explored in detail below.

Many other investment arbitration cases are considered important in understanding the impact that the European Withdrawal has on the protection of investors.

The Spanish Saga cases confirm that the ECT plays an important role in protecting investments in renewable energy.[86] They also provides a "valuable contribution to the analysis of the intersections between investment arbitration tribunals and the EU legal order, as well as the interplay between their case law and the case law of the CJEU,"[87] including the *PV Investors* case or *RREEF* case.[88] There is no unified argument per the disconnection clause,[89] and there is no "absolute monopoly of the CJEU over the interpretation and application of EU law."[90] It is also worth mentioning the *Electrabel* case, where the tribunal concluded that: "EU law would prevail over the ECT in case of any material inconsistency. That conclusion depends, however, upon the existence of a material inconsistency; and the Tribunal has concluded that none exists for the purpose of deciding the Parties' dispute in this arbitration."[91]

State courts are not as sympathetic as arbitral tribunals and take a rather narrow view. A German state court recently granted Croatia's request to declare a pending UN Commission on International Trade Law ("UNCITRAL") arbitration "inadmissible" because the arbitration agreement granted by two EU member states acting as contracting parties to the intra-EU Bilateral Investment

---

available at: https://www.wilsoncenter.org/article/protecting-rule-law-hungary-and-poland (last accessed Jan. 7, 2024).

[86] *See generally* Filip Balcerzak, *Renewable Energy Arbitration – Quo Vadis?, Implications of the Spanish Saga for International Investment Law*, Nijhoff International Investment Law Series, Volume: 23, p. 440.

[87] *Id.* at 91.

[88] *See PV Investors v. Spain*, PCA Case No. 2012-14, Preliminary Award on Jurisdiction (Oct. 13, 2014); *RREEF v. Spain*, ICSID Case No. ARB/13/30, Decision on Jurisdiction of June 6, 2016.

[89] Disconnection clause is understood as provisions that "ensure that between parties to a multilateral treaty which are also parties to a regional organization, the rules of the regional organization prevail over the treaty", see more: *The PV Investors v. Spain*, PCA Case No. 2012-14, Feb. 28, 2020, para. 178; *Charanne v. Spain*, SCC Case No. V 062/2012, Award, Jan. 21, 2016, para. 437.

[90] Filip Balcerzak, *Renewable Energy Arbitration – Quo Vadis?,* Implications of the Spanish Saga for International Investment Law, Nijhoff International Investment Law Series, Volume 23, p. 94.

[91] *Electrabel v. Hungary*, ICSID Case No. ARB/07/19, Decision on Jurisdiction, Applicable Law and Liability (Nov. 30, 2012), para 4.191.

Treaty ("BIT") was invalid.[92]

For the EU and its Member States, legal uncertainty is likely to prevail after withdrawal from the treaty, given the treaty's sunset clause and the risk that tribunals will not recognize the EU's attempt to withdraw from the treaty, as many arbitral tribunal rulings have shown.[93]

In addition to the general legal implications of European Withdrawal, there are also additional implications of discontinuing the ECT. We can learn more about the implication of the European Withdrawal from the notifications regarding the termination of the ECT provided by each country (before the coordinated withdrawal in July 2023 took place).[94] Below is an analyzation of the Polish government notification as an example.

On August 25, 2022, the government of Poland sent a previously approved, but unannounced, bill on the termination of the ECT to the lower chamber ("Sejm").[95] The bill is straightforward, with two Articles – the first gives the President the power to withdraw from the ECT, and the second provides fourteen days for the law to become operative.[96] Moreover, the reasoning can be found in the nine page explanatory note,[97] with the first argument reflecting the position of EU bodies, i.e., the lack of conformity of the ECT with EU law.

---

[92] Filip Balcerzak, *Renewable Energy Arbitration – Quo Vadis? Implications of the Spanish Saga for International Investment Law*, Nijhoff International Investment Law Series, Volume 23, p.161.

[93] Nicholas Lawn & Isabel San Martin, *The End Is Near: The European Commission's Proposed Coordinated Withdrawal from the ECT*, KLUWER ARBITRATION BLOG (July 24, 2023), https://arbitrationblog.kluwerarbitration.com/2023/07/24/the-end-is-near-the-european-commissions-proposed-coordinated-withdrawal-from-the-ect/.

[94] *See e.g.*, Aida Bektasheva, *Withdrawal from the Energy Charter Treaty without its Modernization, or Modernization of the ECT Treaty without Withdrawal by EU Members: What is the Impact of the Two Scenarios?*, INT'L L. BLOG (June 29, 2023), https://internationallaw.blog/2023/06/29/withdrawal-from-the-energy-charter-treaty-without-its-modernization-or-modernization-of-the-ect-treaty-without-withdrawal-by-eu-members-what-is-the-impact-of-the-two-scenarios/.

[95] *Act on the denunciation of the Energy Charter Treaty and the Energy Charter Protocol on Energy Efficiency and Related Environmental Aspects*, drawn up in Lisbon on Dec. 17, 1994, dated Oct. 6, 2022, effective as of Dec. 3, 2022.

[96] Daszko, *supra* note 12.

[97] *Explanatory note to the draft bill on the denunciation of the Energy Charter Treaty and the Energy Charter Protocol on Energy Efficiency and Related Environmental Aspects*, drawn up in Lisbon on Dec. 17, 1994 (Sept. 2, 2022), Sejm of Republic of Poland, Bill No. 2553, available at: https://www.sejm.gov.pl/sejm9.nsf/druk.xsp?nr=2553.

Under the section "Legal Consequences,"[98] Poland also argues that withdrawal from the agreement will not significantly change the situation of foreign investors, as they will continue to be protected by the Polish Constitution, international law, and EU law to the same extent as under the Treaty.

The document further says that the termination will lead to greater legal predictability.[99] However, protection before Polish ordinary courts will not be quick, and the courts may be more sympathetic to the Polish state in these disputes.

Another legal consequence flows from the *Achmea* judgment,[100] which sheds light on the legal future of arbitral awards and whether they will be given in the future under the ETC. The main question concerns the annulment of such awards.[101] The *Achmea* ruling makes clear that annulment will depend on the law in force in the member states concerned, as the provisions of the Treaty on the Functioning of the EU ("TFEU") need not be interpreted as directly affecting the validity or content of a legal act in private law and do not constitute grounds for annulment.[102] It seems that for the duration of the "sunset clause," such a situation will not occur, while after that period, member states will have to deal with this problem.

The legal situation of non-European investors in Europe and their disputes come into question. The Court, in the *Komstroy* case,[103] left open the question of whether extra-EU arbitration under the current EU-Canada Comprehensive Economic and Trade Agreement ("CETA") equally infringes on the jurisdictional autonomy of EU law, as it does in the case of intra-EU arbitration.[104] A close analysis of the CJEU's acceptance of the investment chapter of CETA in Opinion 1/17[105] shows that a positive assessment cannot be easily transferred to the ECT.

B. Social and Economic Implications

The EU member states' notification prior to the European Withdrawal in July

---

[98] *Id.* at 6.
[99] *Id.*
[100] Case C-284/16, *Slovak Republic v. Achmea*, ECLI:EU:C:2018:158 (Dec. 20, 2017).
[101] *Id.* at 4.
[102] Arthur Hartkamp, *Some Practical Consequences of the Achmea Judgement on Intra EU Investment Arbitration*, in NATIONAL JUDGES AND THE CASE LAW OF THE COURT OF JUSTICE OF THE EUROPEAN UNION 198 (Mancaleoni, A.M. & Poillot, E. eds., 2021).
[103] Case C-741/19, *Republic of Moldova v. Komstroy LLC*, ECLI:EU:C:2021:655 (Sept. 2, 2021).
[104] *Id.* at 16.
[105] Opinion 1/17, ECLI:EU:C:2019:341 (Apr. 30, 2019) at ¶ 245.

2023 prompts reflection not only on the legal consequences of withdrawing from the ECT but also on the broader economic and social consequences.

Under the "Economic Consequences",[106] the Polish government pointed out that, based on the "Freedom of Investment Process: Societal Benefits and costs of investor protection in [IIAs],"[107] draft report, the withdrawal will not lead to FDI inflows. Figures showing the correlation between international agreements and FDI inflows yield a variety of results – some show a weak correlation, and others a very strong positive relationship.[108] However, there is a correlation between the scale of FDI and legal regulation in the energy area, where the level of liberalization and maturity of regulation plays a key role.[109] On the other hand, meta-analyses show that the effect of international investment agreements on FDI is so small that it can be considered zero.[110] However, these results do not rule out the possibility that the impact of these agreements is in fact positive, and current research methods are not efficient or precise enough to identify the real effect. As the Organization for Economic Cooperation and Development ("OECD") figures show, the average FDI inflows for the last 10 years in the EU have been 35% of the global economy since 2012 but have declined to 8% of the global economy in the last year.[111] The decrease in percentage coincides with the period of modernization and the beginning of the process of the European Withdrawal.[112]

Moreover, in its notification, the Polish government indicated that savings would be made in relation to the costs of handling ECT-based disputes as a result of the occurrence.[113] Specific amounts were not indicated.[114] Hope remains that

---

[106] *Supra* note 96, at 8.

[107] Joachim Pohl, *Societal Benefits and Costs of International Investment Agreements: A Critical Review of Aspects and Available Empirical Evidence*, (OECD, Working Papers on International Investment 2018/01, 2018).

[108] *Id.* at 19.

[109] TOMASZ BĄK, POTENTIAL IMPACT OF THE ENERGY CHARTER TREATY ON FDI PROMOTION AND PROTECTION IN VIEW OF GLOBAL TRENDS, ENERGY, GOVERNANCE AND POSSIBLE ACTIONS TOWARDS ECT NON-MEMBERS 14 (2013).

[110] Josef C. Brada et al., *Does Investor Protection Increase Foreign Direct Investment? A Meta Analysis*, 35 J. ECON. SURVS., 34, 58 (2020).

[111] *FDI flows, Outward, Million US dollars, Annual, 2005 – 2022*, OECD, https://data.oecd.org/chart/7j93 (last visited Jan. 7, 2024).

[112] *See id.* (showing the decline in FDI flows over the last decade).

[113] *Explanatory note to the draft bill on the denunciation of the Energy Charter Treaty and the Energy Charter Protocol on Energy Efficiency and Related Environmental Aspects*, drawn up in Lisbon on Dec. 17, 1994 (Sept. 2, 2022), Sejm of Republic of Poland, Bill No. 2553, available at: https://www.sejm.gov.pl/sejm9.nsf/druk.xsp?nr=2553; Daszko, *supra* note 12.

[114] *Explanatory note to the draft bill on the denunciation of the Energy Charter Treaty and the Energy Charter Protocol on Energy Efficiency and Related*

these funds will be used for urgent investments in the country.

Finally, the "Social Consequences" [115] include the danger of regulatory chill (reluctance to introduce regulation for the energy sector), which the withdrawal from the ECT will overcome.[116] According to Kyla Tienhaara, "governments will fail to enact or enforce *bona fide* regulatory measures (or modify measures to such an extent that their original intent is undermined, or their effectiveness is severely diminished) as a result of concerns about ISDS."[117]

On the other hand, the EU Commission admitted that the International Treaties contain sufficient guarantees for public interest decision-making that would not be affected.[118] Also, data shows that IIA has a positive impact on regulations in the sense of upholding the rule of law, and in broader scope the regulatory chill is of minor importance.[119]

It is also important to remember that investors often tend to invest abroad, which means that they are not fully familiar with the laws of the country in question. These foreign investors tend to look for a clear and understandable law. Such clear and transparent law attracts investors, whose investments then have a positive impact on economic development.

The European Withdrawal will not only have legal implications for investors. It also affects the social and economic situation worldwide. Therefore, these developments should be watched by all economies of the world, as what happens in the EU can have a real impact on the global economy.

3. How to Fix the European Withdrawal? Legislation Gap Fillers for Investors

The European Withdrawal has entailed further doubts about the level of protection for investors and their investments inside the EU. Legal mechanisms

---

Environmental Aspects, drawn up in Lisbon on Dec. 17, 1994 (Sept. 2, 2022), Sejm of Republic of Poland, Bill No. 2553, available at: https://www.sejm.gov.pl/sejm9.nsf/druk.xsp?nr=2553.

[115] *Id.*

[116] *Id.*; Daszko, *supra* note 12.

[117] Kyla Tienhaara, *Regulatory Chill in a Warming World: The Threat to Climate Policy Posed by Investor-State Dispute Settlement*, 7 Transnat'l Env't L. 229, 233 (2018).

[118] European Commission, *Commission proposes new Investment Court System for TTIP and other EU trade and investment negotiations*, Press release IP/15/5651 (Sept. 16, 2015), available at https://europa.eu/rapid/press-release_IP-15-5651_en.htm.

[119] Filip Balcerzak & Stanisław Drozd, *Human Rights Compatible International Investment Agreements: A Voice from Central & Eastern Europe and Central Asia*, Bus. & H.R. J. 1, 6 (2023).

that remained for investors are "gap fillers" – legal acts operating at the international, regional, and national levels. Below is an overview of the legislation that may be the only hope for investors after the European Withdrawal. The analysis which follows also evaluates the EU's solution to dispute resolution and investor protection.

A. International Regulation

International legal standards provided by the ECT govern the energy market and determine, *inter alia*, relations between countries and investors in terms of international energy trade, energy investments, and the security of energy supplies.[120] Although there are also several provisions of BITs and the obligations arising from those documents, the ECT is the only legal act comprehensive and specific enough to govern the energy market.

What is more, since March 6, 2018 (*Achmea* ruling),[121] investors in the EU are no longer protected by the BITs. Replying to a request for a preliminary ruling from the German Federal Court of Justice, the European Court of Justice assessed the compatibility with EU law of the provisions of the international agreement between Slovakia and the Kingdom of the Netherlands on encouragement and reciprocal protection of investments (BIT).[122] In this case, the dispute between Slovakia and a Dutch company concerned the redressing of a loss caused by amendments to Slovak laws.[123]

Here, it is pertinent to mention the declaration of the European Commission issued to placate investors fearful of the legal consequences of the *Achmea* and following judgments. In its communication on the protection of intra-EU investment,[124] the EU Commission explained, among other things, how the EU protects the rights of investors in the EU and the role of the European Commission in this matter.[125] From the perspective of the energy disputes, the case of *Vattenfall v. Germany*[126] should also be mentioned, where the tribunal held that the *Achmea* decision does not affect their jurisdiction under the Energy Charter Treaty.[127] At the same time, the ruling of the CJEU in the case of *Republic of*

---

[120] *See generally* The Energy Charter Treaty, Dec. 17, 1994, 2080 U.N.T.S. 95.
[121] Achmea, *supra* note 100.
[122] *Id.* at para. 23.
[123] *Id.* at para. 8–9.
[124] *Communication from the Commission to the European Parliament and the Council: Protection of intra-EU investment*, COM (2018) 547/2.
[125] *Id.*
[126] Vattenfall AB v. Federal Republic of Germany, ICSID Case No. ARB/12/12 (May 2012).
[127] *Id.*

Poland vs. PL Holding[128] should also be mentioned. This judgment not only confirmed that intra-EU arbitration is impermissible but also that EU Member States should take action to deter such arbitral proceedings or to prevent the enforcement of their rulings.[129] This has produced results that are evident in the last two verdicts. More recently, on April 19, 2022, the Paris Court of Appeals[130] overturned two intra-EU rulings based on the *Achmea* and *PL Holding* decisions, finding that the tribunals lacked jurisdiction over the claims.[131] This trend continued to grow starting in May 2020, when a majority of EU Member States signed the Agreement for the Termination of Bilateral Investment Treaties between the Member States of the European Union.[132] Therefore, the international bilateral investment treaties protection is no longer a 100% guarantee for investors with the EU.

In a more general legal scope, in terms of the energy trade, the international legal order consists of the provisions of the General Agreement on Tariffs and Trade ("GATT"),[133] which are binding since the WTO agreement incorporating the GATT provisions came into force. Initially, the drafters of the ECT sought a more revised and up-to-date trade regime on which the ECT could be based, thereby paving the way for the adoption of WTO trade provisions (established in 1995) that would replace the outdated GATT provisions and embody the corresponding changes in multilateral trade rules resulting from the Uruguay Round.[134]

The General Agreement on Trade in Services ("GATS") defines the rules for providing services relating to the energy industry.[135] However, there are no

---

[128] Republic of Poland v. PL Holding, CJEU Case C-109/20 (2021).
[129] *See id.*
[130] French Court of Appeal of Paris, Int'l Commercial Chamber, Judgment, Apr. 19, 2022, No. RG 20/14581.
[131] *Id.*
[132] Agreement for the termination of Bilateral Investment Treaties between the Member States of the European Union, May 29, 2020, L 169/1-41.
[133] General Agreement on Tariffs and Trade, July 1986, 1867 U.N.T.S. 187, 33 I.L.M. 1153, available at: https://www.wto.org/english/docs_e/legal_e/gatt47_e.pdf.
[134] *The Trade Amendment (TA) of the Energy Charter Treaty (ECT): Explained to Decision-Makers of Ratifying Countries*, ENERGY CHARTER, at 4, https://www.energycharter.org/fileadmin/DocumentsMedia/Thematic/Trade_Amendment_Explanations-EN.pdf (last visited Apr. 19, 2023).
[135] *The General Agreement on Trade in Services (GATS): objectives, coverage and disciplines*, WTO, https://www.wto.org/english/tratop_e/serv_e/gatsqa_e.htm (last visited Apr. 19, 2024).

separate provisions for the energy sector, and the application of these terms depends on countries' obligations and the content of the appendices.[136] GATS's provisions regulate trade in services in various sectors of the economy and affect energy services.[137]

Moreover, the Paris Agreement implements the United Nations Framework Convention on Climate Change[138] and supplements the Kyoto Protocol,[139] recognizing that renewable energy aims to strengthen the global response to the threat of climate change in the context of sustainable development and efforts to eradicate poverty.[140] However, this agreement does not offer instant remedies for the protecting investments made within the EU.[141]

Hence, the Paris Agreement, Kyoto Protocol, GATT, and GATS are not appropriate legal mechanisms to replace the ECT.

Regarding the protection of human rights, the International Covenant on Civil and Political Rights ("Covenant")[142] provides in Article 2(3) that each signatory is obligated to ensure that "any person whose rights or freedoms as herein recognized are violated shall have an effective remedy."[143] According to Article 14 (1) of the Covenant, "all persons shall [...] be entitled to [...] independent and impartial tribunal established by law."[144]

Despite the fact that the above provisions provide a legal guarantee and have a broad interpretation, they may not provide adequate protection for investors' investments made in the energy sector, which are for specific matters.[145] The aforementioned acts of international law shape the rights and obligations of investors at the general level of law.

Also, although there were many activities and initiatives during the modernization period of the ECT (mentioned in Chapter 2), none of them resulted

---

[136] *Id.*

[137] *Id.*

[138] United Nations Framework Convention on Climate Change, May 9, 1992, S. Treaty Doc No. 102-38, 1771 U.N.T.S. 107.

[139] Kyoto Protocol to the United Nations Framework Convention on Climate Change, Dec. 10, 1997, 2303 U.N.T.S. 162.

[140] Paris Agreement to the United Nations Framework Convention on Climate Change, Dec. 12, 2015, T.I.A.S. No. 16-1104.

[141] *See id.*

[142] International Covenant on Civil and Political Rights, Mar. 23, 1976, 999 U.N.T.S. 171.

[143] *Id.* art. 2(3).

[144] *Id.* art. 14(1).

[145] Natasha A Georgiou, *A modernised ECT reflecting EU values and objectives: a multilateral framework promoting energy investment in a sustainable way?*, EUR. WORLD. Vol. 7(1) (2023).

in a legal act regulating the specific situation of investors in the energy market at a level similar to that of the Treaty.

B. Regional Regulations

The EU itself, which is a main actor leading the European Withdrawal, has several legal mechanisms linked to the protection of investment in the region of the EU.

One such mechanism is the EU's own legislation. On July 23, 2014, the European Parliament and the Council adopted Regulation (EU) No 912/2014 establishing a framework for managing financial responsibility linked to investor-to-state dispute settlement tribunals established by international agreements to which the European Union is party ("EU Regulation 912/2014").[146] The EU Regulation 912/2014 provides for legal actions in two instances – where the respondent is the EU itself and where the respondent is the EU Member State.[147] Despite the fact that the investor-to-state dispute resolution problem is so elaborate and meticulously described, the enormity of the deadlines that the procedure contains comes to mind as a conclusion after reading the act: 15 working days for the notification of the dispute, followed by 45 days for the Commission to decide on the next steps, and 90 days for the Commission to accept the draft agreement prepared by the EU Member State.[148] It is also worth mentioning that Article 6(1) indefinitely includes consultations between the Member State and the European Commission on cooperation, which may affect the duration of the dispute.[149]

A number of cases have arisen on the basis of this legislation. Mention should be made here, among others, of the case of *Prosisa and Risteel Corporation*,[150] in which the company ultimately did not further pursue its claims against the EU.[151] However, there are also less optimistic cases: such as the *Nord Stream 2* case[152]

---

[146] Regulation (EU) No 912/2014 of the European Parliament and of the Council of July 23, 2014, 2014 O.J. (L 257/121-L 257/134).
[147] *Id.* at L 257/122.
[148] *Id.* arts. 8(1), 9(1)(a), 15(3), at L 257/127, L 257/131.
[149] *Id.* art. 6(1), at L 257/127.
[150] Report from the Commission on the European Parliament and the Council on the operation of Regulation (EU) No 912/2014 on the financial responsibility linked to investor-to-state dispute settlement under international agreements to which the European Union is party, at 2-3, COM(2019) 597 final (Nov. 19, 2019).
[151] *Id.* at 3.
[152] *Id.* at 3–4. *Nord Stream 2 AG v. European Union*, PCA Case No. 2020-07, Notice of Arbitration (Sept. 26. 2019), https://pcacases.com/web/sendAttach/11889.

and the *AS PNB Banka* case.¹⁵³ Both cases eventually ended in arbitration but were first approached with the EU Regulation 912/2014,¹⁵⁴ which did not have the expected positive effect.

Another protection mechanism is the European Convention on Human Rights ("ECHR") and its Articles 1, 4, 6, and 14¹⁵⁵ and amendments created in Protocols no. 2, 3, 5, and 8.¹⁵⁶ However, the ECHR contains general, and therefore generic, rights belonging to the individual. The law is not aimed at protecting investments in the energy sector. Furthermore, the protection standards under IIAs provide more specific rules than those for the protection of property rights, life, health, and physical safety in the ECHR. Hence, investors are more likely to refer to the protection standards of investment treaties.¹⁵⁷

The energy market within the EU is also subject to many initiatives, such as the REPowerEU plan,¹⁵⁸ the Clean Energy for All Europeans Package,¹⁵⁹ and the

---

[153] Report from the Commission on the European Parliament and the Council on the operation of Regulation (EU) No 912/2014 on the financial responsibility linked to investor-to-state dispute settlement under international agreements to which the European Union is party, at 4, COM(2019) 597 final (Nov. 19, 2019); *AS PNB Banka v. Republic of Latvia*, ICSID Case No. ARB/17/47 (Dec. 28, 2017), https://icsid.worldbank.org/cases/case-database/case-detail?CaseNo=ARB/17/47.

[154] Regulation (EU) No 912/2014 of the European Parliament and of the Council of July 23, 2014, 2014 O.J. (L 257/121-L 257/134).

[155] Convention for the Protection of Human Rights and Fundamental Freedoms (European Convention on Human Rights, as amended), Nov. 4, 1950, arts. 1, 4, 6, 14, 213 U.N.T.S. 221.

[156] Protocol No. 8 to the Convention for the Protection of Human Rights and Fundamental Freedoms, Mar. 19, 1985, 213 U.N.T.S. 221; Protocol No. 5 to the Convention for the Protection of Human Rights and Fundamental Freedoms, amending Articles 22 and 40 of the Convention, Jan. 20, 1966, 213 U.N.T.S. 221; Protocol No. 3 to the Convention for the Protection of Human Rights and Fundamental Freedoms, amending Articles 29, 30 and 34 of the Convention, May 6, 1963, 213 U.N.T.S. 221; Protocol No. 2 to the Convention for the Protection of Human Rights and Fundamental Freedoms, conferring upon the European Court of Human Rights competence to give Advisory Opinions, May 6, 1963, 213 U.N.T.S. 221.

[157] Iryna Glushchenko, *Human Rights in Investment Claims*, JUSMUNDI (Mar. 13, 2023), https://jusmundi.com/en/document/publication/en-human-rights-in-investment-claims.

[158] *Communication from the Commission to the European Parliament, the European Council, the Council, the European Economic and Social Committee and the Committee of the Regions (REPepowerEU Plan)*, COM (2022) 230 final (May 18, 2022).

[159] European Commission, Directorate-General for Energy, *Clean energy for all*

EU's Energy Union Strategy.[160] The last of the abovementioned contributed to the Energy Union Governance and Climate Action Regulation,[161] which entered into force on December 24, 2018. The regulation emphasizes the importance of achieving the EU's 2030 energy and climate targets.[162] It sets out ways Member States and the Commission should work together to achieve the goals of the energy union.[163] However, the regulation is not geared towards protecting the interests of investors in the energy sector.

The EU is also working on a Multilateral Investment Court ("MIC") to protect investors' rights in a similar way to the ISDS mechanism in the ECT.[164]

C. Multilateral Investment Court ("MCT")

The *Komstroy* case mentioned above is one of the latest steps in a continuing trend in the EU, where the CJEU has extended the views from the *Achmea* case ruling to disputes under the ECT.[165] For nearly a decade, the EU has increasingly and aggressively pursued replacing ISDS with a multilateral investment court to handle investment disputes.[166]

Since 2015, the EU has attempted to institutionalize investment dispute resolution through the creation of the Investment Court System ("ICS").[167] The

---

Europeans (2019), https://data.europa.eu/doi/10.2833/9937.

[160] *Communication from the Commission to the European Parliament, the Council, the European Economic and Social Committee, the Committee of the Regions and the European Investment Bank: A Framework Strategy for a Resilient Energy Union with a Forward-Looking Climate Change Policy*, COM (2015) 080 final (Aug. 28, 2015).

[161] Regulation (EU) 2018/1999 of the European Parliament and of the Council of Dec. 11, 2018 on the Governance of the Energy Union and Climate Action, amending Regulations (EC) No 663/2009 and (EC) No 715/2009 of the European Parliament and of the Council, Directives 94/22/EC, 98/70/EC, 2009/31/EC, 2009/73/EC, 2010/31/EU, 2012/27/EU and 2013/30/EU of the European Parliament and of the Council, Council Directives 2009/119/EC and (EU) 2015/652 and repealing Regulation (EU) No 525/2013 of the European Parliament and of the Council, 2018 O.J. (L328).

[162] *Id.*

[163] *Id.*

[164] *The Multilateral Investment Court Project*, EUROPEAN COMMISSION (modified Jan. 2021), https://policy.trade.ec.europa.eu/enforcement-and-protection/multilateral-investment-court-project_en.

[165] Case C-741/19, *Republic of Moldova v Komstroy LLC*, ECLI:EU:C:2021:655, (Sept. 2, 2021).

[166] *The Multilateral Investment Court Project*, EUROPEAN COMMISSION (modified Jan. 2021), https://policy.trade.ec.europa.eu/enforcement-and-protection/multilateral-investment-court-project_en.

[167] Recommendation of the European Commission for a Council Decision

goal is to create "a single multilateral institution to resolve investment disputes covered by all applicable bilateral agreements," instead of multiple bilateral investment tribunals.[168] As the European Commission points out, a recommendation to the Council of the European Union to negotiate a multilateral court for the settlement of investment disputes[169] can be found in Opinion 2/15 on the exclusive competence of the EU to protect FDI.[170] However, importantly, Opinion 2/15 dealt with extra-EU relations, i.e., EU-Singapore Free Trade Agreement ("EUSFTA").[171]

Although the Council's negotiating directives for a multilateral investment court published on March 20, 2018 ("EU Negotiating Directive")[172] provides some insight into how the multilateral court for the settlement of investment disputes looks, there is still some uncertainty about investor after the European Withdrawal. Although the EU claims that the modernization of the dispute settlement system remains a priority within the evaluation of the ECT, no evaluation of the MCT is available due to the "very recent introduction" of this concept.[173] The EU Negotiating Directive provides, *inter alia*, for a two-tiered judicial system (point 10), independence, even though the members of the court are to be elected by the Member States (point 11), and permanent remuneration for the Court members (point 11).[174] What is also important is that there is no requirement for MIC tribunal members to have experience of or a commitment to policy areas such as climate change.[175]

D. Domestic Regulations

Each EU member state can guarantee appropriate legal solutions to its citizens and investors coming to that country with their investments. The

---

authorizing the opening of negotiations for a Convention establishing a multilateral court for the settlement of investment disputes, COM (2017) 493 final (Sept. 9, 2017).
[168] *Id.*
[169] *Id.* at 4.
[170] Opinion of the CJEU of 16 May 2017, C-2/15, EU:C:2017:376.
[171] *Id.* at 4-5.
[172] *Negotiating directives for a multilateral investment court*, COUNCIL OF THE EUROPEAN UNION (Mar. 20, 2018), http://data.consilium.europa.eu/doc/document/ST-12981-2017-ADD-1-DCL-1/en/pdf.
[173] Recommendation of the European Commission for a Council Decision authorizing the opening of negotiations for a Convention establishing a multilateral court for the settlement of investment disputes, at 4, COM (2017) 493 final (Sept. 9, 2017).
[174] *Id.*
[175] COUNCIL OF THE EUROPEAN UNION, *supra* note 172, art. 10, at 4.

following will focus on the solutions guaranteed by Polish law.

One of the basic guarantees of the Polish legal system is the Constitution.[176] According to the Polish Constitution, investment protection is guaranteed by the right to equal treatment (Article 32), the right to a fair trial (Article 45) or the right to property (Article 64).[177] However, as these are rather universal principles, they will not be able to protect investments made by investors fully effectively.

While Poland is subject to EU law, the EU Commission has stated that the state violates EU law on various issues, including the independence of the judiciary.[178] Poland considers its domestic judicial system and international human rights protection system to be equivalent to investor-state dispute settlement mechanisms under the ECT, while the rule of law has come into question over the past few years.[179] Interestingly, the Polish Constitutional Court even issued a politically charged ruling stating that Article 6(1) of the European Convention on Human Rights is incompatible with the Polish Constitution (Case No. K 7/21),[180] in the aftermath of the ECHR judgments in the case of *Xero Flor v. Poland*,[181] as well as in the case of *Dolińska-Ficek and Ozimek v. Poland*.[182] None of these officially cited reasons seem convincing.

After the European Withdrawal, Poland does not have any comprehensive legal protection for investments in the energy sector. No international, regional, or national regulations will provide effective and complete investment protection.

---

[176] CONSTITUTION OF THE REPUBLIC OF POLAND, Apr. 2, 1997.

[177] *Id.* arts. 32, 45, 64.

[178] David R. Cameron, *EU charges Poland's Constitutional Tribunal with violating EU Law*, YALE MACMILLIAN CENTER (Jan. 3, 2022), https://macmillan.yale.edu/news/eu-charges-polands-constitutional-tribunal-violating-eu-law.

[179] *Press Release, Rule of Law: Commission Issues Recommendation to Poland*, EUR. COMM'N (Jul. 27, 2016) (Memo/16/2644), https://ec.europa.eu/commission/presscorner/detail/en/IP_16_2643; *The Venice Commission Criticizes New Polish Constitutional Tribunal Act*, HELSINKI FOUNDATION FOR HUMAN RIGHTS (Mar. 16, 2016), https://hfhr.pl/en/news/the-venice-commission-criticizes-new-polish-constitutional-tribunal-act.

[180] Case No. K 7/21, Mar. 10, 2022, available at https://ipo.trybunal.gov.pl/ipo/Sprawa?&pokaz=dokumenty&sygnatura=K%207/21.

[181] Xero Flor w Polsce sp. z o. o. v. Poland, App. No. 4907/18 (May 7, 2021), https://hudoc.echr.coe.int/fre#{%22itemid%22:[%22001-210065%22]} (holding that domestic courts had failed under Art. 6 § 1 of the Convention, denying the applicant company a fair trial).

[182] Dolińska – Ficek & Ozimek v. Poland, App. No. 49868/19 and 57511/19 (Nov. 8, 2021), https://hudoc.echr.coe.int/fre#{%22itemid%22:[%22001-213200%22]}.

The situation is also not saved by the concept of the MIC, which has been under development since 2015. However, so far, after 8 years, there has been no effectively established settlement mechanism. A dispute resolution system, such as the one in the ECT (ISDS), is unlikely to be introduced soon.

4. WHAT CAN INVESTORS DO?

Despite the European Withdrawal and the convergence of recent CJEU court rulings, investment arbitration involving EU Member States may not be over. There are practical and instant remedies for investors to overcome the difficult situation they face in Europe with the protection of their investments. Investors may still refer to the litigation finance mechanisms within the 20-year period according to the "sunset clause" or use the corporate structure mechanisms for their companies to protect their investments in Europe.

A. Litigation Finance

Litigation finance can be a support mechanism for those investors who cannot afford to pursue infringement proceedings against their investments. It is a novel activity where financial support is granted to parties in litigation and arbitration proceedings.[183] There are several litigation funders acting on the European market, including Deminor, LitFin – Litigation Financiers, Nivalion AG, Foris AG, and Omni Bridgeway.[184] While each presents different market strategies or operating patterns, they share a common denominator – guaranteeing access to justice. Hence, this solution will work perfectly in the event of a shortage of cash to pursue a dispute.

Investment arbitration could lead to high costs. While the State has financial resources, the investor may be hesitant to initiate the proceedings. The funder is an entity that increases the claimant's chances of winning.[185] The chances can be increased as the litigation funder has financial resources that, unlike the financial capacity of the investor, do not run out quickly.[186] The funder's team works with its expertise to estimate how much of the fund will be necessary for the investment

---

[183] Miltiadis G. Apostoldis, *Third-Party Funding in Dispute Resolution: Financial Aspects and Litigation Funding Agreement*, INT'L HELLENIC UNIV. SCH. OF ECON, BUS. ADMIN. & LEGAL STUD. 6 (Jan. 2017).

[184] *Dispute Resolution Litigation Funding in Europe (Excluding UK)*, LEADERS LEAGUE, https://www.leadersleague.com/en/rankings/dispute-resolution-litigation-funding-in-europe-excluding-uk-ranking-2023-litigation-funders-czechia-germany-france-ireland-netherlands-norway (last visited Jan. 7, 2024).

[185] Daria Davitti & Paolo Vargiu, *Litigation Finance and the Assetization of International Investment Arbitration*, 24 J. WORLD INV. & TRADE 487, 492 (2023).

[186] *See id.*

arbitration.[187]

According to a survey conducted by Woodsford in 2021,[188] 49% of senior financial executives said that their companies "failed to pursue [verdicts] due to cost in 2020," with half indicating claim amounts of $20 million or more.[189] Data shows that investors that are represented by the top tier international law firms with significant expertise in ISDS cases are more likely to win than those not funded by such firms; she similarly found that roughly 61% of them reach a settlement.[190] With litigation funding, investors and their companies can pursue claims and judgments without risk. Losing costs the company nothing, while winning is a financial threat that turns the legal department into a profit generator that adds tremendous value to the company.

B. Corporate Structures

Despite the European Withdrawal, investors may engage in BIT-shopping, virtually relocating their headquarters to countries outside the EU to change the 'nationality' of their investments and thereby access the protection provided by other investment treaties. It remains to be seen whether arbitral tribunals will consistently refuse to exercise jurisdiction if European investors bring claims against European countries or whether non-EU courts will refuse to enforce such awards if investors seek to recover awards against EU member states from assets held in other countries, despite being prohibited from doing so in the EU. In practice, investors may move their seats, use existing seats, or have shareholders bring the claims to continue to be able to bring claims.

As the 2020 study published in the British Institute for Comparative Law stated, "a majority of tribunals find they have jurisdiction despite the respondents' objections to restructuring."[191] Hence, there is a high chance that the use of the

---

[187] *Id.*
[188] 2021 LEGAL ASSET REPORT: A SURVEY OF FINANCE PROFESSIONALS, BURFORD (June 21, 2021), https://www.burfordcapital.com/insights/insights-container/2021-legal-asset-report/ (including responses from 378 senior finance executives, all of whom work for companies with annual revenues of $50 million or more, and most of whom work for companies with annual revenues of $500 million or more).
[189] *See id.* at 15.
[190] GOVEN, BROOKE & JOHNSON, LISE, THE POLICY IMPLICATIONS OF THIRD-PARTY FUNDING IN INVESTOR-STATE DISPUTE SETTLEMENT 25–26 (Colum. Ctr. Sustainable Inv. May 2019), available at https://scholarship.law.columbia.edu/sustainable_investment_staffpubs/8.
[191] EMPIRICAL STUDY: CORPORATE RESTRUCTURING AND INVESTMENT TREATY PROTECTIONS, BRITISH INST. INT'L & COMPAR. LAW 2 (London 2020), https://www.biicl.org/documents/89_biicl-baker-mckenzie-corporate-

change of domicile method may effectively protect investors.

After the European Withdrawal, the remaining signatories include, among others, Japan and Switzerland.[192] It is unlikely that Japan will be the main destination for forum shopping as the arbitration industry does not have a strong presence there.[193] Switzerland, on the other hand, will likely be an attractive destination because it is often chosen as the home of investor-state arbitration and thus has a strong connection to the arbitration industry.[194] As of December 31, 2022, in Switzerland, 40% (18 out of 45) of cases were settled in favor of the investor or settled, of which 15 are disputes involving the EU or EU Member States (4 pending, 3 discontinued, 2 decided in favor of the investor, 4 decided in favor of the state, 1 settled and 1 case which was decided in favor of neither party).[195] While in Japan, there is only one pending case between China and Hong Kong – *Shift Energy v. Japan*.[196] If Switzerland were to remain a contracting party to the imploding ECT and reap the benefits of this by becoming the site of choice for ECT arbitral tribunals – this would expose Switzerland to enormous pressure, that it is not entirely clear whether it can cope with.

Moreover, from a practical standpoint, investors will also have to consider the mechanisms for starting up operations from a third country or the tax rules, which will often require expert knowledge. While structuring through third-country jurisdictions is a solution that can provide investment protection, it is not a solution that promotes even economic development in the region. It can contribute to more effective investment protection in the EU.

5. CONCLUSIONS

"Making accurate predictions is difficult – especially when it concerns the

---

restructuring-and-investment-treaty-protections-2020.pdf.

[192] *Contracting Parties and Signatories of the Energy Charter Treaty*, INT'L ENERGY CHARTER, https://www.energychartertreaty.org/treaty/contracting-parties-and-signatories/ (last visited Mar. 25, 2024).

[193] Hiroyuki Tezuka & Yutaro Kawabata, *Arbitration Guide Japan*, INT'L BAR ASS'N (Jan. 2018), https://www.ibanet.org/MediaHandler?id=DBCF3CAB-E985-4A9B-BBA1-D8D9D191EF5E.

[194] Matthias Scherer, *Arbitration Guide Switzerland*, INT'L BAR ASS'N (Jan. 2018), https://www.ibanet.org/MediaHandler?id=8DA26206-5B7E-49A5-A69F-4BEF37D6408A.

[195] *Investment Dispute Settlement Navigator Switzerland*, UNICITAD, https://investmentpolicy.unctad.org/investment-dispute-settlement (last visited Jan. 7, 2024).

[196] *Shift Energy Japan KK v. Japan*, initiated in 2020, UNICITAD, https://investmentpolicy.unctad.org/investment-dispute-settlement/cases/1194/shift-energy-v-japan (last visited Jan. 7, 2024).

future. These words, attributable to an anonymous futurologist, come to mind when reflecting on the state of announced withdrawals from the ECT." [197]

Two dates –November 24, 2022 and July 7, 2023 – have made history in the energy sector. However, it is not only the ECT modernization process, but also EU case law that has led to the current situation. The ECT denunciation process has left investors in Europe less optimistic than they might have been. There were a number of interesting solutions in the ECT modernization procedure that were likely to stick. In principle, the EU managed to renegotiate many of the issues that were required. Nevertheless, the European Withdrawal was the chosen one.

European Withdrawal has legal implications, namely limited legal protection before international arbitral tribunals based on the legal principles of the ECT (sunset clause), usually weaker and questionable legal protection provided by the national legal system, and a lack of legal certainty, with the risk of future annulment of arbitral awards by national courts.

There are also social and economic implications, mainly the decline in foreign investment inflows caused by the international dispute settlement crisis, which may have a prominent impact on the global economy.

After all, the ECT remains a unique multilateral platform that provides legally binding provisions on a wide range of energy issues. Negotiating such a treaty was only possible because of the political strength of the post-Cold War 'window of opportunity.' Such an opportunity is unlikely to be repeated any time soon and may appear to be a real strategic mistake for the EU to simply throw in the towel now.

By leaving the ECT, EU investors lost protection for new investments in countries such as Turkey, Central Asia and the South Caucasus. For the rest of this decade, investment in alternatives to Russian fossil fuels will remain crucial, as will reliable and uninterrupted transit through the Southern Gas Corridor, which the Treaty's transit provisions also cover. Hence, finally, the European Withdrawal may be an opportunity for other non-EU countries that choose to fill the investment vacuum in Europe – not waste such an opportunity to take the lead.

However, the question remains whether to continue with a legal framework that prioritizes investment protection and arbitration in times of unprecedented transition and uncertainty or whether other instruments are more appropriate to spur a clean energy transition. This creates another question about the meaning and purpose of European Withdrawal. Still, EU regulations and the idea of how to structure the judicial system are vague. Foreign investments undertaken in the EU are an important part of the energy sector.

---

[197] Jan Klabbers, *A Moral Holiday: Withdrawal From the Energy Charter Treaty*, ESIL REFLECTIONS (Dec. 15, 2022), https://esil-sedi.eu/esil-reflection-a-moral-holiday-withdrawal-from-the-energy-charter-treaty/.

Investors are therefore left with 'alternative solutions' such as, *inter alia*, supporting themselves with external funding (to initiate infringement proceedings on investments already made) or structuring the company in investment-friendly jurisdictions. In the coming years, investors will have to adjust their investment strategies and decisions to avoid the negative consequences of the European Withdrawal. Not only should Europeans' eyes be wide open, but the world should observe the progress with the European Withdrawal, as it may have a serious impact on the global economy.

GOLDMAN SACHS 1MDB ARBITRATION

BENIN LEE*

In early October 2023, Goldman Sachs Group, Inc. ("Goldman Sachs") filed a suit against the government of Malaysia in the London Court of International Arbitration ("LCIA").[1] This developing case provides valuable insights into contemporary arbitration developments while spurring discourse on the advantages of LCIA arbitration and the strategic decisions made in international arbitration.

The lawsuit relates to a major financial scandal involving Goldman Sachs and the Malaysian state-owned investment fund 1Malaysia Development Berhad ("1MDB"). The scandal came to light in 2015, leading to investigations in multiple countries.[2] 1MDB acquired substantial funds through bond issuances made between 2009 and 2013,[3] intended for investment initiatives and collaborative ventures. According to the United States ("U.S.") Department of

---

*Benin Lee is a recent graduate from the American University Washington College of Law, where he served as a former Articles Editor of the Arbitration Brief. Benin is interested in international trade and its overlap in governance and international relations. Additionally, he is particularly fascinated with the utilization of alternative dispute resolution ("ADR") mechanisms to effectively resolve conflicts between state and private actors. Currently, Benin is clerking in the Baltimore City Circuit Court, where he continues to refine his legal skills and gain practical experience.

[1] *Goldman Sachs sues Malaysia over 1MDB settlement*, REUTERS (Oct. 11, 2023), https://www.reuters.com/markets/asia/goldman-sachs-sues-malaysia-discord-over-1mdb-settlement-escalates-2023-10-11/.

[2] Bradley Hope, Tom Wright, & Patrick Barta, *How a Malaysian Scandal Spread Across the World*, WALL STREET J. (Dec. 12, 2016), https://www.wsj.com/graphics/1mdb-how-a-malaysian-scandal-spread-across-the-world/.

[3] *Explainer: Goldman Sachs and its role in the multi-billion-dollar 1MDB scandal*, REUTERS (Oct. 12, 2023), https://www.reuters.com/markets/asia/goldman-sachs-its-role-multi-billion-dollar-1mdb-scandal-2023-10-12/.

Justice, 1MDB redirected $4.5 billion[4] of these funds to offshore accounts and shell companies. Malaysian authorities contend that additional billions remain untraceable in the ongoing investigation.[5]

Goldman Sachs, a New York City-based financial institution, and its Malaysian subsidiary were involved in the scandal because of their role in underwriting 1MDB's bond deals.[6] In October 2020,[7] Goldman Sachs admitted to conspiring to violate the Foreign Corrupt Practices Act ("FCPA") in a scheme that involved paying over $1 billion in bribes to Malaysian and Abu Dhabi officials to obtain lucrative business.[8] Of the billions 1MDB made from the scandal, Goldman Sachs earned hundreds of millions in fees.[9]

As a part of the guilty plea, Goldman Sachs entered into a deferred prosecution agreement[10] with the U.S. Attorney's Office for the Eastern District of New York and the Department of Justice's Criminal Division, Fraud, and Money Laundering and Asset Forfeiture sections. According to the terms of these agreements, Goldman will be subject to a criminal penalty and disgorgement—made to surrender ill-gotten gains— totaling over $2.9 billion.[11] Additionally, the bank reached parallel settlements domestically and internationally,[12] with authorities in the United Kingdom, Singapore, Malaysia, and others.

The parallel agreement between Goldman Sachs and the Government of Malaysia stated that, if the Malaysian government did not receive at least $500 million in assets and proceeds by August 2022, Goldman Sachs must make a one-time interim payment of $250 million.[13] The interim payment remains the point of contention in Goldman Sachs's arbitration claim in which Goldman Sachs argues that Malaysia violated its obligations to appropriately credit assets against

---

[4] *Id.*
[5] *Id.*
[6] *Id.*
[7] *Press Release: Goldman Sachs Charged in Foreign Bribery Case and Agrees to Pay Over $2.9 Billion*, U.S. DEP'T OF JUSTICE OFFICE OF PUBLIC AFFAIRS (Oct. 22, 2020), https://www.justice.gov/opa/pr/goldman-sachs-charged-foreign-bribery-case-and-agrees-pay-over-29-billion.
[8] *Id.*
[9] *Id.*; *see also* Norman Goh, *Malaysia's 1MDB Task Force Calls Goldman Arbitration Move 'Premature,'* NIKKEI ASIA (Oct. 12, 2023), https://asia.nikkei.com/Spotlight/Society/Crime/Malaysia-s-1MDB-task-force-calls-Goldman-arbitration-move-premature.
[10] *See Press Release: Goldman Sachs Charged in Foreign Bribery Case and Agrees to Pay Over $2.9 Billion*, *supra* note 7.
[11] *Id.*
[12] *Id.*
[13] REUTERS, *supra* note 1.

the guarantee provided in the settlement agreement.[14]

Conversely, Malaysia's Attorney General Chambers argued that Goldman Sachs's allegation "mischaracteri[z]es the conduct of the government."[15] The 1MDB task force formed by the Malaysian government has accused Goldman Sachs of attempting to divert attention from the late interim payment, the due date of which Goldman Sachs has already asked for an extension several times.[16]

According to the task force, Goldman Sachs brought this dispute to arbitration only after the Malaysian government threatened to sue. Goldman Sachs's choice of arbitration in the LCIA was a strategic decision based on the forum's unique benefits. If Goldman Sachs had not initiated arbitration proceedings in the LCIA, the Malaysian government could have referred the dispute to a different arbitration body, such as the International Chamber of Commerce or the International Centre for Dispute Resolution.[17]

The first of the LCIA's unique benefits is its reliability and establishment. Formally inaugurated in 1892, this court has over 120 years of history.[18] The long history allows parties to predict how their disputes will be settled reliably. The reliability of the LCIA provides a diverse array of professional experience and expertise, which has granted it the respected title of the "commercial 'world court.'"[19] The body hears multiple claims a year for countries worldwide.

In addition to its reliability, arbitration in the LCIA is highly efficient compared to other arbitration establishments.[20] This increased efficiency is

---

[14] Valeria Martinez, *Goldman Sachs Sues Malaysia Over 1MDB Scandal Settlement: Reports Disagreement Over 2020 Settlement*, INVESTMENT WEEK (Oct. 12, 2023), https://www.investmentweek.co.uk/news/4133672/goldman-sachs-sues-malaysia-1mdb-scandal-settlement-reports.

[15] Rozanna Latiff, *Malaysia Denies Goldman Sachs' Allegations in 1MDB Arbitration Suit*, REUTERS (Oct. 12, 2023), https://www.reuters.com/markets/asia/goldman-sachs-sues-malaysia-discord-over-1mdb-settlement-escalates-2023-10-11/.

[16] *Id.*

[17] *Id.*

[18] *History*, LONDON CT. OF INT'L ARB., https://www.lcia.org/lcia/history.aspx (last visited May 6, 2024).

[19] Thomas Lehmann & Erdem Evranos, *LIDW 2022: What is the Role of London for North American Disputes? A North American Perspective on London as an International Dispute Hub*, KLUWER ARB. BLOG. (May 11, 2022, 11:47 AM), https://arbitrationblog.kluwerarbitration.com/2022/05/11/lidw-2022-what-is-the-role-of-london-for-north-american-disputes-a-north-american-perspective-on-london-as-an-international-dispute.

[20] *LCIA*, LINKLATERS, https://www.linklaters.com/en/knowledge/topics-hub/toolkits/dispute-toolkit/arbitration/arbitral-institutions-and-clauses/lcia (last visited May 6, 2024).

partially because the LCIA does not require terms of reference.[21] The terms of reference in an arbitration agreement prevent the parties from introducing claims beyond the scope of the terms and limit the procedural and substantive rules used in the debate.[22] Although terms of reference can be beneficial, reaching a preliminary agreement on them can be arduous and time-intensive.

Additionally, the final awards at the LCIA are binding on the parties and parties generally waive their right to appeal.[23] Because the final award is not reviewed, parties can rest assured that they will not risk their award being overturned and will avoid the cost of repeat arbitration.

The LCIA's reputation for efficiency continues regarding the cost of arbitration. While other arbitration institutions base fees on the amount in dispute or the complexity of the issues at hand, LCIA calculates arbitration costs and arbitrator's fees at an hourly rate.[24] Therefore, parties may find arbitrating in the LCIA cheaper when the amount in controversy is excessive.

Lastly, the LCIA is unique in its commitment to confidentiality. Article 30.1 provides that LCIA cannot publicize any documents relating to the arbitration, the award, or the outcome without the agreement of all parties.[25]

The LCIA offers distinct advantages to Goldman Sachs by providing a strategic edge in various aspects. The first key advantage lies in the stringent confidentiality it ensures. Despite Goldman Sachs being a publicly traded company, the LCIA empowers the firm with increased control for managing or mitigating any adverse exposure during the proceedings.[26] Secondly, the efficiency of the LCIA facilitates a swift resolution process, allowing Goldman Sachs to secure a final award without relinquishing a substantial portion of the disputed amount in arbitration fees. Consequently, irrespective of the case's

---

[21] *See generally* LCIA ARBITRATION RULES 2020.

[22] *Arbitration: Terms Of Reference*, BODENHEIMER, https://www.changing-perspectives.legal/arbitration/frequently-arising-issues-in-international-arbitration/terms-of-reference/#:~:text=The%20Terms%20of%20Reference%20are,in%20regard%20to%20procedural%20matters (last visited May 6, 2024).

[23] Julia Bihary & Alexis L. Namdar, *Head-to-Head: Comparing Three Arbitration Regimes for US Based Asset Managers*, PROSKAUER (Aug. 31, 2022), https://www.mindingyourbusinesslitigation.com/2022/08/head-to-head-comparing-three-arbitration-regimes-for-us-based-asset-managers/.

[24] *Id.*

[25] LCIA ARBITRATION RULES 2020, art. 30.

[26] *Frequently Asked Questions*: *26. Is the Final Outcome of an Arbitration Made Public?*, THE LONDON CT. OF INT'L ARB., https://www.lcia.org/Frequently_Asked_Questions.aspx (last visited May 6, 2024).

outcome, opting for the LCIA as the seat of arbitration enables Goldman Sachs to avoid both high costs and negative publicity associated with the arbitration process.

In conclusion, although the case between Goldman Sachs and the Malaysian government continues, Goldman Sachs may have gotten the initial upper hand by submitting the complaint to the LCIA.

NAVIGATING POLICY SHIFTS IN INVESTOR-STATE DISPUTE SETTLEMENT IN LATIN AMERICA: A CASE STUDY OF COLOMBIA

JAKE HELFANT*

States have historically utilized provisions for Investor-State Dispute Settlement ("ISDS") to secure foreign investment by ensuring that disputes with foreign enterprises are governed and processed outside of the jurisdiction of sovereign states.[1] International Investment Agreements, including Bilateral Investment Treaties ("BITs") and investment chapters within Free Trade Agreements ("FTAs"), typically contain ISDS provisions that often mandate arbitration through the International Center for Settlement of Investment Disputes ("ICSID")–an institution part of and funded by the World Bank.[2] These provisions disadvantage states because they prohibit governments from initiating proceedings against foreign investors and make it challenging for states to assert counterclaims on the merits.[3] More than 150 countries have signed and ratified the ICSID convention, subjecting certain investment claims to the procedural

---

*Jake Helfant is a law student at American University Washington College of Law with a keen interest in investor-state dispute settlement. He serves as the Article Editor and Treasurer of The Arbitration Brief and is a member and Treasurer of the Alternative Dispute Resolution Honor Society.

[1] *See Primer on International Investment Treaties and Investor-State Dispute Settlement*, COLUM. CTR. ON SUSTAINABLE INV., https://ccsi.columbia.edu/content/primer-international-investment-treaties-and-investor-state-dispute-settlement (last visited May 7, 2024) (discussing how a common rationale for investment treaties that often contain ISDS provisions is to attract foreign investment, though evidence that such agreements increase foreign investment inflows is inconclusive).

[2] *ICSID and the World Bank Group*, ICSID, https://icsid.worldbank.org/about#:~:text=ICSID%20is%20one%20of%20the,Investment%20Guarantee%20Agency%20(MIGA) (last visited May 7, 2024). *See Investor-State Dispute Settlement in Latin America and the Caribbean*, CTR. FOR ADVANCEMENT RULE L. AMS., GEO. L., https://isdslac.georgetown.edu/ (last visited May 7. 2024).

[3] *Investor-State Dispute Settlement in Latin America and the Caribbean*, *supra* note 2.

rules and regulations and institutional support of ICSID.[4]

As of November 2023, twenty-two Latin America & Caribbean ("LAC") states have been subject to over 400 investor-state disputes, with the majority of LAC states facing claims under ISDS provisions.[5] Arbitral panels issued over 175 awards in these cases, ruling in favor of investors in about half of them and in favor of states in the other half.[6] Notably, cases involving Argentina, Venezuela, Peru, Mexico, and Ecuador have contributed over 95% of total award and settlement costs in LAC, while European and North American companies account for over 83% of investment claims brought against LAC states.[7]

ICSID faced a significant legitimacy crisis following a series of cases brought against Argentina after the country's financial crisis of the early 2000s.[8] The set of cases settled through ICSID during these years arguably had "'very different interpretations of the law and diametrically opposed holdings,'" calling into question the viability of the ICSID arbitral system.[9] From 2007 to 2012, Bolivia, Ecuador, and Venezuela all withdrew from the ICSID Convention, attributing their withdrawals to the institution's preference for transnational corporations over states and their citizens.[10]

In recent years, companies have successfully brought numerous ISDS claims against Colombia, Peru, and Mexico. Colombia's endorsement of thirteen new BITs and eight new FTAs between 2005 and 2015, which authorized ICSID arbitration, led to increased claims against the country.[11] Indeed, all twenty-one ICSID arbitrations against Colombia were registered after 2015.[12] The "Mining & Quarrying" industry has ultimately emerged as the most involved sector in

---

[4] *Database of ICSID Member States,* ICSID, https://icsid.worldbank.org/about/member-states/database-of-member-states (last visited May 7, 2024).
[5] *Investor-State Dispute Settlement in Latin America and the Caribbean, supra* note 2.
[6] *Id.*
[7] *Id.*
[8] Gary Born & Claudio Salas, *Chapter 1: Exploring Latin America's ICSID Arbitration Landscape,* at 9–12, in LATIN LAWYER, THE GUIDE TO INTERNATIONAL ARBITRATION IN LATIN AMERICA (José Astigarraga ed., 2d ed. 2023).
[9] *Id.*
[10] *Id.*
[11] *Id.; International Investment Agreements Navigator,* UNCTAD, https://investmentpolicy.unctad.org/international-investment-agreements/countries/45/colombia (last visited May 7, 2024) (filter for "Colombia" in "IIAs by Economy").
[12] *Cases,* ICSID, https://icsid.worldbank.org/cases/case-database (last visited May 7, 2024) (filter for "Colombia" in "Respondent(s) Nationality(ies)").

Colombia's ICSID cases.[13]

Following Gustavo Petro's narrow victory in the May 2022 Colombian elections, in which Petro became the country's first leftist president, Colombia potentially entered a new ISDS policy era.[14] Colombia may follow in the footsteps of Bolivia, Ecuador, and Venezuela by relinquishing its obligations under the ICSID Convention. Colombia is not the only LAC country considering denouncing the ICSID Convention.[15] Honduras is currently facing a claim from an American company for around $11 billion, prompting the Central American nation to reassess its commitments to the ICSID.[16]

Petro's administration, seeking closer ties with Venezuela, signed a BIT with its neighbor in early 2023–the first BIT signed by Venezuela since 2008.[17] The agreement reflects Venezuela's denunciation of the ICSID Convention, providing that disputes between investors and the host state may be resolved in the host state's domestic courts or submitted for resolution under the 1976 UNCITRAL Arbitration Rules.[18] The Colombia-Venezuela BIT also heightens the threshold for corporations seeking to bring claims against host states by implementing more restrictive ISDS provisions, including a narrower definition of 'investment', increased regulatory deference for states, and a shorter sunset clause.[19] Through this agreement, Petro's administration displayed a willingness to include alternative mechanisms for dispute resolution in future investment treaties, and perhaps abandon the ICSID Convention entirely.

Despite concerns about nationalization under Petro's administration, the

---

[13] *Industries Involved in Disputes*, CTR. FOR ADVANCEMENT RULE L. AMS., GEO. L., https://isdslac.georgetown.edu/industries-most-involved-2/ (last visited May 7, 2024).

[14] The Associated Press, *Former Rebel Gustavo Petro Wins Colombia's Presidential Election*, NPR (June 19, 2022), https://www.npr.org/2022/06/19/1106118791/tight-colombian-runoff-pits-former-rebel-millionaire.

[15] *See, e.g.*, *Honduras Threatens ICSID Withdrawal Over $11 Billion 'Neo-Colonial' Special Economic Zone Claim*, BRETTONWOODS PROJECT (July 19, 2023), https://www.brettonwoodsproject.org/2023/07/honduras-threatens-icsid-withdrawal-over-11-billion-neo-colonial-special-economic-zone-claim/.

[16] *Id.*

[17] Christian Leathley, Daniela Paez, & Lucila Marchini, *Colombia and Venezuela Agree a New Bilateral Investment Treaty, Venezuela's First Since Withdrawing from the ICSID Convention*, HERBERT SMITH FREEHILLS (Mar. 14, 2023), https://hsfnotes.com/latamlaw/2023/03/14/colombia-and-venezuela-agree-a-new-bilateral-investment-treaty-venezuelas-first-since-withdrawing-from-the-icsid-convention/.

[18] *Id.*

[19] *Id.*

president assured the public that his vision for Colombia did not include expropriation.[20] Petro prioritizes a transition from fossil fuels, despite oil and coal production making up around half the value of the country's exports.[21] Though Petro has not stated how his administration will bring about this economic and energy transition, expropriation or burdensome environmental standards would likely result in further ICSID claims. In March 2023, 220 organizations–including environmental interests and labor unions–urged withdrawal from certain international investment treaties.[22] These organizations argued that decisions made by ICSID arbitral tribunals often favor corporate interests at the expense of human rights and environmental protection.[23]

Based on the Colombia-Venezuela BIT, it remains likely that the Petro administration will exclude ICSID provisions in any new BITs or FTAs it signs. Colombia may consider withdrawing from current BITs and FTAs or explore the possibility of negotiating exclusions of ICSID provisions. However, denouncing the ICSID Convention might prove politically challenging given Petro's broader policy ambitions in the energy and healthcare space, and his relatively low approval rating.[24] Even if Petro denounces the ICSID Convention, Colombia remains bound to the institution for the foreseeable future due to existing BITs, FTAs, and ongoing disputes under the ICSID Convention. However, the future trajectory of ISDS in LAC remains uncertain. Given the growing calls for states to exit current investment treaties due to concerns over labor standards, climate change, and alleged bias against state parties, substantial reforms may be necessary for the long-term viability of ISDS, particularly the ICSID, in the LAC region.

---

[20] Manuel Rueda, *Colombian Candidate Says He Won't Nationalize Property*, AP NEWS (Apr. 18, 2022), https://apnews.com/article/business-colombia-presidential-elections-economy-south-america-9970507b92a233017c3c22c14977c06f.
[21] Alice Hancock, Ian Johnston & Joe Daniels, *Petro courts foreign investors to fulfil Colombia's 'potential' beyond oil*, FIN. TIMES (July 18, 2023), https://www.ft.com/content/fe2113c1-a128-49a4-b4fc-8282e66aee67.
[22] *Over 220 Organizations Call on Colombian Government of Gustavo Petro and Francia Márquez to Withdraw from International Investment Treaties that Enable Million-Dollar Corporate Claims*, INST. FOR POL'Y STUD. (Mar. 7, 2023), https://ips-dc.org/release-over-220-organizations-call-on-colombian-government-to-withdraw-from-international-investment-treaties/.
[23] *Id.*
[24] Hancock et al., *supra* note 21.

ARBITRATION AT THE ILO: A NEW MECHANISM

YONAH WASIK*

In over 100 years of international arbitration, courts have settled only one labor arbitration case. In April 2013, the Rana Plaza Factory in Dhaka, Bangladesh, collapsed and killed over 1,100 workers in the garment industry, injuring many more.[1] By 2018, the Permanent Court of Arbitration ("PCA") oversaw and settled the first international labor arbitration between two global unions and a private entity, regarding the collapse.[2] Numerous declarations from the International Labour Organization ("ILO") assert that the lack of international arbitration comes not from the absence of international agreements on labor standards, but because a mechanism that can hold multinational corporations accountable to the ILO's international standards does not exist.[3] Currently, the ILO can hear twenty-five cases against state parties each year through the Committee on the Application of Standards ("CAS").[4] However, that mechanism lacks enforceability and can only review a limited number of cases. Other options include numerous international arbitration courts, such as the PCA or the International Chamber of Commerce ("ICC"), but these options are costly and more specialized in investor-state relations than international labor law.[5] Therefore, an arbitral mechanism at the ILO could better effectuate worker

---

*J.D. Candidate at American University Washington College of Law; Contact: yw2242a@american.edu

[1] *The Rana Plaza Disaster Ten Years on: What Has Changed?*, ILO (Apr. 2023), https://www.ilo.org/infostories/en-GB/Stories/Country-Focus/rana-plaza#intro.

[2] *Bangladesh Accord Arbitrations*, PERM. CT. ARB., https://pca-cpa.org/en/cases/152/ (last visited May 6, 2024).

[3] *See* Walton Pantland, *SPECIAL REPORT: How Can We Build an International Labour Court?*, INDUSTRIALL UNION (Aug.17, 2022), https://www.industriall-union.org/special-report-how-can-we-build-an-international-labour-court.

[4] Karon Monaghan, *The Committee of Experts on the Application of Conventions and Recommendations: The Centenary Year*, 32 KINGS L. J. 197, 199 (2021).

[5] *See What is the Average Cost of an International Arbitration?*, MOLOLAMKEN (2021), https://www.mololamken.com/knowledge-what-is-the-average-cost-of-

justice.

The CAS is a standing body of representatives from states, employers, and worker delegates that reviews and discusses a report from a committee of experts at the International Labor Conference each year.[6] The CAS is the closest thing to an enforcement body at the ILO, and it focuses on twenty-five or fewer cases in which states are non-compliant with ILO conventions.[7] It then presents non-compliant states with recommendations and support. For example, in 2023 the CAS evaluated Afghanistan's poor treatment of women and children in almost every industry and sector.[8] The CAS and all its members acknowledged the extreme decline in protections and rights of women and children in the labor force since the Taliban took control in 2021, but it did no more than condemn the Taliban's actions and urge them to stop their discriminatory and violent practices.[9]

The CAS's sole enforcement mechanism is "naming and shaming" non-compliant states to encourage states to apply ILO conventions.[10] Experts widely regard this as ineffective in securing rights and protections for the world's laborers for various reasons.[11] First, the CAS may only hear a limited selection of cases. Also, the CAS may only hear cases against states and cannot hear complaints from individuals, classes, or unions.[12] Lastly, there is no guarantee that a state will take CAS's recommendations or comply with ILO conventions.[13] Perhaps most concerning is that the CAS does not have the capacity or ability to hear cases against corporations.[14] If the CAS could apply its "naming and shaming" powers to cases against corporations, it could coerce some states into providing greater

---

an#:~:text=Investors%20pursuing%20arbitration%20under%20investment,the%20procedural%20choices%20parties%20make%20.l.

[6] *Conference Committee on the Application of Proceedings (ILC 2022),* ILO (Oct. 10, 2022), https://www.ilo.org/global/standards/applying-and-promoting-international-labour-standards/conference-committee-on-the-application-of-standards/WCMS_857921/lang—en/index.htm#:~:text=The%20Conference%20Committee%20on%20the,Application%20of%20Conventions%20and%20Recommendations.

[7] *See* Monaghan, *supra* note 4, at 199.

[8] *See* Int'l Labour Org., *Record of Proceedings*, at 70–75, ILC.111/Record No. 4B/P.II (July 17, 2023), https://webapps.ilo.org/wcmsp5/groups/public/---ed_norm/---relconf/documents/meetingdocument/wcms_888016.pdf.

[9] *See id.*

[10] *See, e.g., id.* (condemning Afghanistan's violation of ILO Convention No. 111).

[11] *See, e.g.,* Jean-Michel Servais, *The Right to Take Industrial Action and the Supervisory Mechanism Future*, 38 COMP. LAB. L. & POL'Y J. 375, 389 (2016) (discussing how the ILO can only encourage compliance with ILO conventions).

[12] Pantland, *supra* note 3.

[13] Monaghan, *supra* note 4, at 199.

[14] Pantland, *supra* note 3.

remedial measures to individuals. Under the current structure, individuals are unlikely to receive aid even if a state follows the CAS's legislative and administrative recommendations.

International courts of arbitration have different capabilities than the CAS. For example, the PCA, the London Court of Arbitration, and the International Chamber of Commerce provide a venue for arbitration for individuals, states, and corporations.[15] In the past couple of decades, global unions have pushed for global collective bargaining with multinational corporations using Global Framework Agreements ("GFAs").[16] This kind of organization allowed for the Rana Plaza case at the PCA and could conceivably make arbitration courts a viable option for protecting the rights of workers. However, there are two major problems with this strategy. First, arbitration can be expensive.[17] Such an expense could be burdensome for a growing global union. Worse, corporations may avoid signing GFAs.[18] Because corporations from states like the United States and the People's Republic of China avoid signing GFAs, individuals often lack the opportunity to bring their cases before a court of arbitration.[19] This results in a patchwork of courts that are nowhere near accessible enough to workers attempting to protect their rights around the globe.

An arbitral mechanism at the ILO could fix some of the problems posed by the currently available mechanism by combining the enforcement power of arbitral courts alongside the political power of the ILO.[20] The ILO could use its standard-setting power to encourage more states to enforce the use of GFAs and access to global unions. This would likely slowly expand the reach of global unions and increase the accessibility of arbitral courts. An arbitral mechanism hosted by the ILO would then be able to hear a wide range of cases from individuals, states, and corporations in a forum specialized to handle labor disputes. Due to its specialty, the mechanism at the ILO would likely be less costly and more effective. Scholars recognize governments should initially focus on expanding GFAs and domestic legislation to increase the power of global unions, but access to a less expensive and specialized mechanism could better effectuate justice for workers around the globe.[21]

---

[15] *The Main Institutions of International Arbitration*, COOLEY (July 31, 2023), https://www.cooley.com/news/insight/2023/2023-07-31-the-main-institutions-of-international-arbitration.
[16] Pantland, *supra* note 3.
[17] *See id.*
[18] *Id.*
[19] *Id.*
[20] *Id.*
[21] *Id.*

Made in the USA
Middletown, DE
19 September 2024